Deployed

Steps of Hope in Times of Uncertainty

ALSO BY BRENDA PACE

Journey of a Military Wife

Dedicated: Steps of Faith in God's Plan
Devoted: Steps of Love Toward Healthy Relationships
Deployed: Steps of Hope in Times of Uncertainty
Directed: Steps of Peace in Times of Transition

Medals Above My Heart: The Rewards of Being a Military Wife
(Coauthored with Carol McGlothlin)

The One Year Yellow Ribbon Devotional: Take a Stand
in Prayer for Our Nation and Those Who Serve
(Coauthored with Carol McGlothlin)

Deployed

Steps of Hope in Times of Uncertainty

BRENDA PACE

AMERICAN BIBLE SOCIETY

Philadelphia

DEPLOYED: STEPS OF HOPE IN TIMES OF UNCERTAINTY
(JOURNEY OF A MILITARY WIFE SERIES)

By Brenda Pace
Edited by Peter Edman, Davina McDonald, and Stacey Wright

ISBN 978-1-941448-59-5
ABS Item 124540

Design by Jordan Grove
Cover image by Frankie Aryee

Set in Arno Pro and Avenir

American Bible Society
101 North Independence Mall East
Philadelphia, PA 19106

www.american.bible

Printed in the United States of America

Contents

Journey 1:
Deployed, Not Despondent 7

Journey 2:
Reunited and Resilient 73

An online version of JOURNEY OF A MILITARY WIFE is also available. You can find this book series, small group study guides, and a place to invite others to share this journey with you at www.MilitaryWife.bible.

Journey 1

Deployed, Not Despondent

Introduction

Military personnel preparing to deploy sometimes receive from the chaplain a camouflage bandana printed with the words of Psalm 91. It serves as a reminder of God's promised presence during deployment:

> *He who dwells in the shelter of the Most High*
> *will abide in the shadow of the Almighty.*
> *I will say to the LORD, "My refuge and my fortress,*
> *my God, in whom I trust."* (Psalm 91:1–2)

Psalm 91 encourages trust in the Lord in all circumstances. It is a promise of help in times of trouble. The words paint a picture of God's faithfulness as a large freestanding shield that hides and protects the whole person.[1]

I wonder, where is the bandana for me as a deployed wife? Truthfully, I want more than a bandana. I want a blanket to cover me, transforming my fear to faith, my stress to strength, and my despondence to delight.

Of course, no such blanket exists, but God's Word points me to the one who provides such covering. God's Spirit breathes life into the words of Scripture and there I find hope and help for the situations I face. The words of the Bible are not just history lessons; they are living words that can transform minds and hearts.

The book of Exodus is the account of Moses leading the Israelites on a type of deployment. While not exactly like the circumstances of a deployed wife, it holds many truths that may apply to the journey. For the next thirty days, as we walk with the Israelites, listen to the orders the Lord gave them and heed the guidance the Lord may have for you. The promise of his presence in the middle of your situation is as true today as it was for the Israelites in the desert.

Each day, you will find a devotional waypoint. A *waypoint* is a stopping place on a journey. It is a single specific location. Waypoints may be places to which you want to return, or they may be significant landmarks. The waypoints you encounter on this thirty-day journey will help you focus prayerfully on a theme, question, or topic that can enhance your dedication to God and your understanding of God's purpose for you. Start each day with this prayer from Psalm 119:18. *Lord, "Open my eyes, that I may behold wondrous things out of your law."*

Why not join with some fellow sojourners to study God's Word together? As a companion to this book you will find online at www.MilitaryWife.bible a set of Bible studies complete with leader and participant notes to guide your discussion.

Welcome to the journey!

Waypoint 1

Dear Deployment

Read

And [the Lord] said, "My presence will go with you, and I will give you rest." (Exodus 33:14)

Reflect

Dear Deployment,

While this is not your first visit to our family, fourteen months will certainly make it the longest. As we near our first month together, I want to share a few thoughts with you. As expected, you've come bearing "gifts"—loneliness, anxiety, fatigue, frustration, hectic schedules, sleepless nights, even a broken window and dishwasher. The thing is, my God has also offered some gifts of his own—reminders of his presence in the midst of the journey. After just one month, I can already see how he intends to use your stay to change our family, to teach us, to help us grow and mature in him.

I know the blessings of God's gifts will far exceed the annoyances of yours. So, deployment, while I cannot say that I am happy you are here, and I certainly do not enjoy your company, you are welcome to stay. I know that we will have some difficult days together, and honestly, I hope that once you leave, I will never have to see you again.

More than anything, I choose to trust my God. I know when the appointed time comes for you to leave, my family and I will be able to say with certainty born of experience that God really does cause all things to work together for the good of those who love him and are called according to his purpose (Romans 8:28). We will declare we really can do all things through Christ who gives us strength (Philippians 4:13). Yes, we will see the glory of God through this and we will say, "Thank you!"

With regards,

Tracie

Air Force wife Tracie penned these words to a personified deployment. I read them and shook my head in wonder. What journey did this young woman take to get to the place where she could see deployment as good and describe it as a blessing?

Tracie would be the first person to tell you the blessing of deployment was hard-earned, born out of persevering through loneliness and fighting through fear. She would tell you she did this well on some days and not so well on other days. Most importantly, she would tell you that she did not get to the place of blessing alone. Tracie had the help of family, friends, and military agencies. Her key source of help was the presence of God, who walked with her during the time her husband was away.

The book of Exodus chronicles a type of deployment. Though different from the deployment you may face as a military wife, you can apply the biblical principles presented. The deployment described in Exodus was the first of this type for the Israelites. They were not sure what their journey would hold. No doubt they wondered if they would even continue to exist as a people. They had no resource guides or agencies to look to for assistance. They did not have friends who had walked the road before. This was a maiden voyage. They learned some valuable first-person lessons that can benefit those who are looking toward, or are in the midst of deployment.

Just like Tracie, the Israelites made it through deployment primarily with the presence and help of the Lord. That same help and presence of the Lord is available to you as you make your deployment journey.

Respond

What are words you would use to describe how you feel about deployment? Take a moment to write the words in a journal. Consider using the words as the basis of a prayer asking God to help you view deployment through a lens of blessing.

Prayer for the journey

Father, I look to you as my help and my hope. I ask you to help me view my circumstances through a lens of blessing and gratitude. Grow my faith as I daily trust you. Amen.

Waypoint 2

Burning bush orders

Read

> And the angel of the LORD appeared to him in a flame of fire out of the midst of a bush. He looked, and behold, the bush was burning, yet it was not consumed.... When the LORD saw that he turned aside to see, God called to him out of the bush, "Moses! Moses!" And he said, "Here I am." (Exodus 3:2–4)
>
> "Come, I will send you to Pharaoh that you may bring my people, the children of Israel, out of Egypt." (Exodus 3:10)

Reflect

Deployment begins long before military personnel depart from home base. Deployment begins with notification. Notification is that time when an official alert travels through the chain of command and the preparation to mobilize is set in motion. The word itself, let alone the act, can challenge the most organized, test the most patient, and discombobulate the most confident. The notice usually comes during an ordinary day, in the midst of mundane activity—and it gets our attention!

God sent deployment orders to Moses at just such a time. On an ordinary day, while shepherding a flock of sheep for his father-in-law, the Lord spoke to Moses from a burning bush. Say, what? You read it right—we are talking flames of fire from a burning, but not burned, bush!

In Scripture, fire is often a sign of God's presence. There is no doubt fire and smoke draw attention.[2] On this day, God certainly got Moses' attention when he did not allow the fire to consume the wood. Such an unnatural event could not happen unless God made it happen. God demonstrated that he could make the ordinary into something extraordinary.

When Moses turned his attention to the burning bush, the voice of God instructed him to remove his shoes. Again, God made something ordinary become something extraordinary when a common plot of ground became a sanctuary.[3]

God may not speak to you in a burning bush, but you can be sure he wants to get your attention. Are you open to hear God's voice? As you face this deployment, look to God to demonstrate himself in your life in an extraordinary way. He wants to help turn ordinary times and places into sacred times and places that remind you he is present.

Respond

Think of a time when God got your attention. What were the circumstances? What made you aware of him? When has God transformed your ordinary day or place into something extraordinary?

Prayer for the journey

Father, as I go through an ordinary day, I pray for an awareness of your presence. Open my eyes to see you. Open my ears to hear you. Help me pay attention and respond to you today. Amen.

Waypoint 3

The dreaded 'D' word

Read

> But Moses said to God, "Who am I that I should go to Pharaoh and bring the children of Israel out of Egypt?" (Exodus 3:11)

Reflect

The very word "DEPLOYMENT" can strike fear into the heart of the bravest and most independent military spouse. Deployment can mean a call to guard a hostile border, battle militant terrorists, combat illegal drugs, and fight deadly disease. Any complaint or protest invites the response: "You should have known what you were getting into" or "Don't be surprised, this is what you signed up for." When deployment orders arrive, the last thing I want to hear is, "Put on your big-girl panties and deal with it." Give me time. I will get there. *(O Lord, please let me get there!)*

Another dreaded D word that can accompany deployment is doubt. My personal deployment convoy included a line of doubts about my ability to navigate the terrain ahead.

Sister, you can take comfort in the fact that a number of biblical heroes started out struggling with doubt when their orders arrived. We remember Moses as a powerful leader who performed miraculous events with the anointing of God. When God gave him his deployment orders, however, Moses doubted his ability to accomplish the mission. The book of Psalms holds some deep expressions of doubt. David, one of Israel's greatest and most courageous heroes, wrote many of the Psalms.

Consider these words of doubt from his hand:

> *How long must I take counsel in my soul and have sorrow in my heart all the day? How long shall my enemy be exalted over me?* (Psalm 13:2)
>
> *I had said in my alarm, "I am cut off from your sight . . ."* (Psalm 31:22)
>
> *O Lord, how many are my foes! Many are rising against me; many are saying of my soul, there is no salvation for him in God.* (Psalm 3:1–2)

When you read the above Psalms in their entirety, you see that though David questioned God's presence, he did it from the perspective of knowing this truth: God *was* present. Even though things around or within were not as they should be, God was with him. He took his doubts to the source of his hope. In his honesty, he found a deeper relationship with God. The psalms written by David do not end with doubt—they end with hope.[4]

If you think about it, we always judge heroes for where they end up, not where they start. Doubts at the beginning of deployment do not have to end up as defeat at the end of deployment. Instead, God can transform such doubts into maturity and confidence.

Respond

What doubts might you have concerning the challenges ahead? Heroes such as Moses and David doubted. How do these examples encourage you? Read Psalm 13 and write in a journal what you learn about doubt and hope.

Prayer for the journey

Lord, in the midst of my doubts and fears, remind me of your steadfast love. I confess my doubts to you and ask you to strengthen my faith. Amen.

Waypoint 4

Power of attorney

Read

> God also said to Moses, "Say this to the people of Israel, 'The LORD, the God of your fathers, the God of Abraham, the God of Isaac, and the God of Jacob, has sent me to you.' This is my name forever, and thus I am to be remembered throughout all generations." (Exodus 3:15)

Reflect

I watched my husband pack his rucksack before he deployed. The list was specific and the task was straightforward. The list included particular items of necessity—clothing, toiletries, and military equipment.

I like lists. A list can remove emotion and turn an unpleasant event into a task. Tasks have measureable outcomes. Tasks have points of completion.

A deployment checklist for a military spouse is not items to purchase but rather tasks to complete. Even then, it can read like a cut and dry list of to-do's by which to place a big red checkmark. You can throw yourself into completing a task and not have to think about the purpose—just get 'er done!

- ☑ Obtain power of attorney
- ☑ Organize financial details
- ☑ File automobile information
- ☑ Update will

The most important item on my deployment checklist was probably the power of attorney. When my husband gave me a power of attorney, it gave me the authority to act in his name on his behalf.

In a way, God gave Moses a power of attorney to act on behalf of the Lord. Moses would take the name of the Lord with him when he told the Jewish leaders God's plan to deliver them from bondage. Moses would show his power of attorney to Pharaoh in the form of supernatural acts when he acted on behalf of the Lord in telling Pharaoh, "Let my people go!" God's name would be the credentials Moses needed to give him courage and comfort.[5]

A power of attorney issued in the authority of her husband's name can bring a sense of courage and comfort for legal matters to a deployed wife. Jesus wants you to have courage and comfort by using the credentials of the power of attorney he has given us in his Word, when he said, "Whatever you ask in my name, this I will do, that the Father may be glorified in the Son" (John 14:13).

Respond

What does it mean to you to see prayer as having a power of attorney? Read these verses and meditate on the power that is in the name of Jesus: Mark 16:17–18, Acts 3:6, Philippians 2:9–11.

When we pray in Jesus' name, we pray with spiritual authority, inheritance and might. Jesus' death on the cross, and subsequent resurrection, was a powerful sacrifice. It is our inheritance. Therefore, we boldly approach God because of Jesus' gift. It is a gift that keeps on giving—through you and through me. My prayers are to reflect the character, nature, and purpose of Christ.

Prayer for the journey

Thank you, Jesus, for making it possible for me to come to you in prayer. Help me as I go through each day to make you a priority. I do not want to add time with you as just another item on my to-do list. It is a gift and a joy to spend time with you. I want to feel your presence. I depend on the strength you provide. Thank you for being present and accessible. Amen.

Waypoint 5

Plagued by delays

Read

> Then Moses turned to the Lord and said, "O Lord, why have you done evil to this people? Why did you ever send me? For since I came to Pharaoh to speak in your name, he has done evil to this people, and you have not delivered your people at all." (Exodus 5:22–23)
>
> Then the Lord said to Moses, "Pharaoh's heart is hardened; he refuses to let the people go." (Exodus 7:14)

Reflect

He is packed. There are red check marks indicating the completion of the preparation checklist. You have accepted that deployment is a reality, but he is still here. It seems like the deployment will never happen. If he has to go, then go already! The sooner he goes, the sooner he will return, right?

Welcome to the "*hurry up and wait*" syndrome that pokes fun at the military's penchant to rush toward readiness only to sit for long periods before action. When it happens to you, it is not at all funny. The tendency seems like a paradox to what we characterize as a methodical and mechanized military.

The military helps drive home a true-life lesson: We cannot control time and what happens within the boundaries of time. Who can set the time when a storm may destroy a home? When a son or daughter falls in love? When an illness strikes? When a child takes a first step? We cannot control many things—good or bad. Yet we can have confidence that God is with us at all times.

When you are ready to get deployment started (so it can end!), it is hard to enjoy the wait. The Israelites certainly were not enjoying their wait, as the cruel bondage they experienced got worse. Scripture does not give a timeline for the events of Exodus, but we can surmise it took more than a few weeks from orders to exit. The timing was in God's hands. He said *go* and it would happen, but it was not as simple as packing up one day and leaving the next. Even God's presence did not guarantee instant results.[6]

What did Moses do in his time of waiting? "Moses turned to the LORD ..." (Exodus 5:22). In private, he took his discouragement to God. His words indicate he thought God's promised deliverance would happen faster and with greater ease. You can hear the frustration and disappointment in his words: "and you have not delivered your people at all" (Exodus 5:23b).[7] Moses needed the strength and courage such communion with God would provide. If you read ahead in Exodus 7, you see their exit would literally be plagued by delays.

The lesson on timing is an important one in the context of deployment—and life. Events do not always happen on our timetable. Plans change. Other considerations affect our schedule, and no matter how meticulously we plan, we cannot control time.

Respond

How does waiting cause you to doubt God's faithfulness? What can you do to counteract doubt?

Prayer for the journey

Lord, give me patience to wait and trust in your timetable. Remind me of your Word: "Do not to be anxious about tomorrow, for tomorrow will be anxious for itself. Sufficient for the day is its own trouble" (Matthew 6:34). Amen.

Waypoint 6

Soul preparation

Read

> The blood shall be a sign for you, on the houses where you are. And when I see the blood, I will pass over you, and no plague will befall you to destroy you, when I strike the land of Egypt. (Exodus 12:13)

Reflect

How do I prepare for a separation that will take my beloved thousands of miles and countless imaginable dangers away? I can check off lists until the red ink in my pen is finished and still not be prepared in the way that counts. How do I prepare my soul for such a departure? There is no formula to make the gut-wrenching farewell easy. There are no pat answers to alleviate fears of the unknown.

Oh, that the angel of the Lord could put blood on my doorpost to be sure death would pass by our home. There would be no fearful anticipation of a knock on the door and the words, "We regret to inform you …"

When it comes to deployment, the elephant in the room is the anticipatory grief that takes up residence in your soul. Your fear of what could happen becomes your new reality.

Actual blood on my doorframe has no power to deter death today, just as it had no actual power to deter death for the Israelites. For them, the presence of blood painted on the top and sides of the door was a testimony to the faith of those who dwelled in the home.[8] For the Israelites, God's promise to *"pass over"* them ensured their physical protection.

Today, I cannot control what will happen to my family or me. However, I can protect my soul as I practice trusting in Jesus. Jesus, the Lamb of God who gave his life for us, redefined Passover to be an eternal protection. Whether you walk out the door to deploy, or you simply go to the grocery store, you can be confident of this eternal protection. The person who trusts in Christ can be certain that death and the grave will not overcome.

Respond

Passover is a Jewish observance characterized by careful preparations.[9] What preparation have you made for your soul-care as you approach this deployment?

Prayer for the journey

Father, you have called me on this journey and I want to trust you for every step. Help me trust you for the protection of my family—both now and for eternity. Amen.

Waypoint 7

Wheels up

Read

> Then he summoned Moses and Aaron by night and said, "Up, go out from among my people, both you and the people of Israel; and go, serve the LORD, as you have said." (Exodus 12:31)

Reflect

"Wheels up" and "underway" are terms used by military personnel to describe that time when the plane is in the air or the ship is out to sea. Now the deployment countdown can really begin. For Moses and the Israelites the term could have been "Roll out" to mean it was time to roll the wheels of the carts out of Egypt and into the desert.

A core theme of the journey the Israelites took out of Egypt is that of leaving an undesirable situation for one that is better.[10] You may say, "I don't need to leave an unacceptable situation and go to something better. I certainly do not see deployment that way. Deployment *is* the undesirable situation!"

I get it! But, what if you could view this time when your husband is away as a time to make something better? Is there anything you can leave—something you are accustomed to that you could improve? Might this be a time to become healthier? Could you use some of the extra deployment pay to pay off debt? What special memories can you make with your children? In other words, what can you do that does not just pass the time, but actually brings improvement to your life?

Historians record the exodus as the time when the Hebrews gained their freedom. While that is true, their exit was not to gain freedom for freedom's sake. Their exit was to gain freedom to worship and serve the Lord.[11] Their exit gave them an opportunity to expand the name of the Lord.[12] Their exit was an opportunity for God to teach them about himself and their relationship with him.[13]

Respond

Consider planning your own "Wheels Up/Underway" Day. Make the day of departure a day to do something positive. Start "Day One" with a good choice. How might deployment be a time to make a major positive change in your life? In a spiritual sense, how might you serve the Lord during this time of deployment? How might you "expand the name of the Lord" during deployment?

Prayer for the journey

Lord, let this time of deployment for me and other military sisters be a time of growth. Show me areas where I can become stronger in my character and in my faith. Amen.

Waypoint 8

Remember this day

Read

> Then Moses said to the people, "Remember this day in which you came out from Egypt, out of the house of slavery, for by a strong hand the LORD brought you out from this place." (Exodus 13:3a)

Reflect

Stories before bedtime, prayers at meals, when you put up or take down your Christmas tree, certain things you do on a family vacation, are rituals. Rituals form family identity. Rituals give us a sense of belonging and make us feel safe.

As the Israelites left Egypt, God directed Moses to initiate specific rituals by way of feasts and festivals. To this day, the Jewish faith observes these rituals, thus emphasizing the importance of remembrance and the value of tradition. Such rituals help create meaning and structure in life.

Rituals can help you navigate a successful deployment. They can act as the glue that keeps you connected to your husband, family, friends, and God. For the military family walking through deployment, rituals can serve as a bridge that narrows the distance. In a practical way, they can:

- Strengthen family connections
- Give children a sense of security by knowing what to expect, and when
- Give a family its own personality and sense of being unique and special
- Reinforce a family's values
- Help family members cope during challenging times.[14]

Deployment is not a time to suspend family rituals, but to continue them and even come up with some new ones to practice during separation. Remember that the ritual comes in the actual doing of an activity. The ritual is the act. Moses did not just tell the people to remember; the remembering was in the act of the feasts and festivals God had him establish.

Respond

What are some of your family rituals? How do these strengthen your relationships? What are some rituals of faith you can establish during this time of deployment?

Prayer for the journey

Father, I pray you will strengthen our family during times of separation. Keep our family strong and together. Strengthen our ties with one another and with you. Give us joy, laughter, and sweet memories as we celebrate special rituals and family traditions. Amen.

Waypoint 9

Unexpected detours

Read

> When Pharaoh let the people go, God did not lead them by way of the land of the Philistines, although that was near. For God said, "Lest the people change their minds when they see war and return to Egypt." But God led the people around by the way of the wilderness toward the Red Sea. (Exodus 13:17–18a)

Reflect

The Israelites left Egypt, but the direction God sent them was neither the fastest, nor the easiest. Scripture tells us God led them by way of an unexpected route to protect them. He knew armies would attack and such direct conflict would surely bring discouragement.[15]

Kristen Welch writes about such unexpected detours in her book *Rhinestone Jesus:*

> … I think most of us view roadblocks in our path of life as setbacks. These obstacles alter our journeys and leave us discouraged. But God provides detours if we pay attention. When we choose to see His alternate route as an opportunity for something new rather than a dead end, it shifts our perspective.[16]

We have to be careful not to discount a detour. Instead, look to see if the detour is actually something God is doing because he knows what is best. Though we may never know the precise timing in all these things, we can have confidence that God knows how to work all things together for our good.

Just because the road is more difficult does not mean it is not God's best way. Think about the difficulty of childbirth, or getting in shape. Such challenges are painful, but can end up producing good in and for us. Deployment can certainly be a painful, out of the ordinary situation; but if God is involved, the chances of it being something good are much better!

Respond

In what ways is it difficult for you to view deployment or other challenging situations as something God can use for good? Can you think of times in your life when a detour ended up being a blessing?

Prayer for the journey

Father, I do not like detours and places where I cannot see the road ahead. Help me not to whine or bemoan difficult places, but rather trust that, because you are present, you will bring something good from the experience. Amen.

Waypoint 10

A bag of bones

Read

> Moses took the bones of Joseph with him, for Joseph had made the sons of Israel solemnly swear, saying, "God will surely visit you, and you shall carry up my bones with you from here." (Exodus 13:19)

Reflect

It is tempting to overlook a seemingly odd and morbid passage of Scripture that talks about carrying a bag of bones on a journey, but that would be a mistake. This little verse tucked into Exodus 13 has great meaning. This little verse is a statement of connection. It connects the past to the present and the present to the future. This little verse is a statement that lets us know this exodus out of Egypt is part of God's larger plan for the Israelites.[17]

The book of Exodus is a continuation of the story started in Genesis. God delivered his people out of bondage not because they deserved it, but because of a promise made to Abraham who carried it to his son Isaac, who carried it to his son Jacob, who carried it to his son Joseph. Later, Joseph requested the Israelites take his bones to Canaan when they finally left Egypt (Genesis 50:24–25).[18] The promise to make the Israelites a nation in the land of Canaan was a promise that captivity in Egypt would not thwart. The bones of Joseph represented a commitment by the people to trust God for their past, present, and future.

It is easy to view deployment with tunnel vision and to forget that, from a military and national perspective, a larger plan is at work. Whatever your thoughts or feelings about that military or national plan, the challenge I offer you today is to view it from a personal perspective. Believe that God can use deployment to fulfill the larger plan for your life.

Think about it: long before Moses led the Israelites out of the country, before they became slaves, even before they grew into a nation of millions in Egypt, Joseph's inspiration already indicated that God had a grand strategy both for going into Egypt and coming out of Egypt. Over the four-hundred-year period that Israel was in captivity, it was easy to lose sight that there would be deliverance.

When the Israelites were struggling in mud quarries making one brick at a time, no doubt it was hard to see that God had a larger plan. They were just trying to make it through one day at a time. When your house is a mess, your kids are sick, and stacks of dishes are in the sink, it is hard to see how God is at work on a larger plan for your good. *But:* don't forget where the bones are buried, because you will get to dig them up and carry them out. What kind of bones will you carry out?

Respond

In what ways might difficult circumstances be part of a larger plan for your good? Joseph's bones were tangible symbols of his faith that someday the circumstances for the Israelites would get better. What bones of hope and faith are buried in your life and family? Do you have relatives that have buried a legacy of faith in you? If possible, contact a loved one or dear friend and talk about your shared faith and hope.

Prayer for the journey

Lord, give me a hope greater than this day. Give me a hope that sees beyond the activity of the present. Give me a hope that is more than a wish, but is a strong bridge that carries me from today into tomorrow. Amen.

Waypoint 11

Cloudy with a chance of guidance

Read

> And the LORD went before them by day in a pillar of cloud to lead them along the way, and by night in a pillar of fire to give them light, that they might travel by day and by night. The pillar of fire by night did not depart from before the people. (Exodus 13:21–22)

Reflect

Cloudy days are reason enough for me to stay in my pajamas and curl up on the couch for a Netflix marathon. I do not need any other excuse. I can use clouds as a reason to put off errands that I need to do, and even cancel appointments that have been on the books for months. I can let lingering clouds affect my emotions. The longer they hang around, the darker my mood can grow.

As I read Exodus, I noticed that clouds did not bring about depression, excuses, or binge TV watching. In fact, when you see the word cloud, you can bet that God's presence is in or near that cloud. This discovery is making me view cloudy days through a different lens.

The Israelites may not have known where they were as they traveled in the wilderness, but they did have a guide. The Lord provided them with shade from a pillar of cloud by day and light from a pillar of fire by night. Whenever and wherever the cloud moved, they were to follow. Knowing where they were going was less important than knowing who they were following.[19] The cloud was a physical sign of the Lord's presence. He did not leave them, day or night. His presence was to show them the way.[20] If they kept their eyes fixed on the cloud, they would not be lost.[21]

Respond

What triggers you to experience a dark day? Why is knowing where you are going less important than knowing whom you are following? Write out Hebrews 12:2 and put it in a place to remind you of the need to keep your eyes on Jesus:

> . . . let us strip off every weight that slows us down, especially the sin that so easily trips us up. And let us run with endurance the race God has set before us. We do this by keeping our eyes on Jesus, the champion who initiates and perfects our faith. . . . (Hebrews 12:1–2, NLT)

Prayer for the journey

Lord, set my spiritual compass toward you. Help me see your presence even on the cloudiest of days. Amen.

Waypoint 12

Shut up and stand up

Read

> When Pharaoh drew near, the people of Israel lifted up their eyes and behold, the Egyptians were marching after them, and they feared greatly. (Exodus 14:10a)
>
> And Moses said to the people, "Fear not, stand firm, and see the salvation of the LORD, which he will work for you today. For the Egyptians whom you see today, you shall never see again. The LORD will fight for you, and you have only to be silent." (Exodus 14:13–14)

Reflect

I know this waypoint carries a bold title, but in essence, this is what God, through Moses, said to the Israelites. God was not speaking to comfort troubled, anxious hearts. No, he spoke to motivate weak, pathetic faith.[22] God brought the children of Israel out of Egypt because he heard their cry for help and deliverance. They did not get very far before they lifted different cries.

It is easy for me to identify with the Israelites. Put me in a precarious situation and my imagination can take off in all kinds of unhealthy directions. I then just need a swift kick in the rear to help me get a grip and to jolt me into reality, as Moses did by telling the Israelites to "stand firm and shut up!"

Here is the twist: The Israelites were afraid of the Egyptians. These were the same Egyptians the Israelites lived with and around for hundreds of years. The Israelites may have felt anger and frustration toward their taskmasters, but never this kind of fear. Why? They had never seen the Egyptians come against them as a hostile army. They knew the sting of their whips, but now they faced the point of their spears.

All of a sudden, the Israelites viewed themselves as weak in the face of the Egyptian army who could destroy them. The Egyptians did not present themselves as such a threat until the Israelites deployed out of Egypt.

Sister, do you see the connection? Challenges present themselves in a different way during this season of deployment. Existing situations may now become threats as they awaken weakness. Some of your *same* may begin to look very *different* during deployment.

You may have experienced anxiety, temptation, or feelings of hopelessness before, but deployment can make them look darker, and more difficult to overcome. The circumstances at home and your surroundings may not have changed, but they can present in a different way because of your husband's absence. Guard yourself against thin-skinned faith and know the Lord can fight for you. Just as he drowned the Egyptian threat, he can drown the anxiety that can control you, the temptation that can destroy you, and the hopelessness that can defeat you.

I am not going to tell you to shut up, but I am going to encourage you to fear not and stand firm!

Respond

How have you experienced your "same" looking "different" during difficult seasons such as deployment? What are some ways you can guard against "thin-skinned faith?"

Prayer for the journey

Help me to be strong and courageous. Deliver me from fear and discouragement. Remind me that you are my God and you are with me wherever I go (Joshua 1:9). Amen.

Waypoint 13

Go forward!

Read

> The LORD said to Moses, "Why do you cry to me? Tell the people of Israel to go forward. Lift up your staff, and stretch out your hand over the sea and divide it, that the people of Israel may go through the sea on dry ground. And I will harden the hearts of the Egyptians so that they shall go in after them, and I will get glory over Pharaoh and all his host, his chariots, and his horsemen. And the Egyptians shall know that I am the LORD, when I have gotten glory over Pharaoh, his chariots, and his horsemen." (Exodus 14:15–18)

Reflect

I do not swim well. In a pool, I stay close to the edge so I can quickly grab it if I feel like I might sink. That edge means safety to me.

I wonder how many of the Israelites could not swim well. The Israelites faced the challenge of walking through walls of water with no edge to hold on to and no defensive shield to hold the water back. My response would be: Push me, carry me, or knock me out, then tell me when we are on the other side.

I have felt overwhelmed when my husband has been deployed. On those days, I wished someone could just knock me out and revive me when it was over. Melodramatic, yes. Honest, yes. I did not want to think about a tidal wave of loneliness that could crush me, a wave of responsibility that could engulf me, or a tsunami of fear that could overpower me.

You have to sometimes overcome what should be a natural fear. The Israelites did not have to make the entire journey to the Promised Land through walls of water, but the first part of the journey presented a huge challenge. They had to take a step of trust. They faced a legitimate fear. If anyone could stand frozen in fear, it was these sojourners. Except, God was the one who held the walls of water from overtaking them.

Some days of deployment will bring more struggle than other days. The sad truth is that we often bow *out* of the struggle before we gain the strength that can come *from* the struggle. Hard things can produce strength, and struggle is an essential ingredient of any forward movement.

Just as the Lord released the water at just the right time to drown the enemies of Israel, he can drown your fears and your discontentment. He can drown anything that may threaten your personal victory in him. With God, you can move forward. Do not abandon the struggle too soon.

Respond

What is your natural response to struggle? What are you learning as you ride out the wave of struggle?

Prayer for the journey

Lord, do not let me give up too soon. Help me to persevere through the struggle knowing you are ever present to guide me, sustain me, and help me grow. Amen.

Waypoint 14

Break out in song!

Read

> Then Moses and the people of Israel sang this song to the LORD, saying, "I will sing to the LORD for he has triumphed gloriously; the horse and his rider he has thrown into the sea." (Exodus 15:1)
>
> Then Miriam the prophetess, the sister of Aaron, took a tambourine in her hand, and all the women went out after her with tambourines and dancing. (Exodus 15:20)

Reflect

May I tell you a secret? Singing has helped get me through deployment. It is true. I love to sing. I am one of those people who need to carry a sign that reads: *Caution! Will Break Out in Song!*

However, I did not sing during the early months of my husband's first deployment. I did not even sing sad songs. Then, one day, while reading Psalm 59, my eyes fell on these words:

> But I will sing of your strength;
> I will sing aloud of your steadfast love in the morning.
> For you have been to me a fortress
> and a refuge in the day of my distress.
> O my Strength, I will sing praises to you.
> for you, O God, are my fortress,
> the God who shows me steadfast love.
> (Psalm 59:16–17)

That same day, after reading this psalm, I contacted a friend who also enjoyed singing. I suggested we get together and sing! We pulled a couple of other deployed spouses in with us. Before that deployment was over, our little group sang in chapel and at a couple of formal military events. Singing became a type of celebration for what God had done, what he was doing, and what he was going to do in our lives. Personally, singing helped me keep my focus on God and gave voice to my faith and hope.

The songs of Moses and Miriam gave voice to the faith of the Israelites. They celebrated the end of their captivity, but they also celebrated the hope of what was to come.[23] I smile when I read of Miriam teaching the song of praise to all the women. The journey was not over; in fact, it had just started, but they sang a song of celebration.

Sister, do not miss the importance of celebration. Celebrate every victory. Build celebration into your schedule. You made it through the first day of deployment—celebrate! You made it through the first month of deployment—celebrate! You ate one piece of chocolate cake instead of the whole cake—celebrate!

Oh, there will be a celebration when your husband gets off the plane, but until then, sing in the face of fear and declare hope and trust for the future.

So sing, sister, sing! Sing in the shower. Sing in your car. Sing and be reminded that God is your fortress, is your refuge, and daily shows you his steadfast love!

Respond

Listen to a song that uplifts you and whether you can carry a tune or not, sing along!

Prayer for the journey

"I will sing to the Lord as long as I live; I will sing praise to my God while I have being. May my meditation be pleasing to him, for I rejoice in the Lord" (Psalm 104:33–34). Amen.

Waypoint 15

When the song becomes a grumble

Read

> Then Moses made Israel set out from the Red Sea, and they went into the wilderness of Shur. They went three days in the wilderness and found no water. When they came to Marah, they could not drink the water of Marah because it was bitter; therefore it was named Marah. And the people grumbled against Moses, saying, "What shall we drink?" (Exodus 15:22–24)

Reflect

Wait a minute. Hold the presses. Didn't we just make a big deal about singing and celebrating? Forget about *my* tendency to do a quick about face from singing to grumbling; what about God's chosen people? God just delivered these folks from slavery and then brought them face to face with a water wall miracle. Do you find it ironic that these folks grumbled over water when they just saw what God did with an entire sea?

We often describe times of difficulty, discouragement, or spiritual dryness as a desert place. We may have just experienced a spiritual high, only to come face to face with the frustrations of life. I can personally testify that my most common response in these times is to complain and question God's goodness.[24] *Complain* sounds so much better than *grumble*, right? Grumbling was also the response of the Israelites when their circumstances did not match up to their expectations.

Here is the thing: complaining is not necessarily a bad thing. Corporations, businesses, and even the military have systems in place to receive complaints in order to make improvements in their practice. However, the complaints of the Israelites had nothing to do with a desire to make things better. The complaints that came from their mouths were indicative of the lack of faith in God found in their hearts. Theirs was rebellious complaining.[25]

Sister, do not miss the profound lesson in the simple way this situation was resolved. Are you paying attention? Do you hear a drum roll? Here it is: The solution came in a simple piece of wood. Read it for yourself: "And he cried to the LORD, and the LORD showed him a log, and he threw it into the water, and the water became sweet" (Exodus 15:25a).

The answer to their complaints was right there all the time. They just needed the Lord to show them.

I don't know about you, but I would trip over that log. I would walk around that log. I might even pick it up and try to use it for decoration. I would not think to use it to change my circumstances. Without the Lord, the log would have just been a piece of wood on the path. With the Lord, the log became a means to bring refreshment.

When complaint moves to grumbling, it indicates my lack of faith in God to bring about a solution. Grumbling is a product of looking at my circumstances instead of looking to God.[26] Desert places can test my faith and obedience, but God will guide me if I listen to him and walk in obedience to his commands (Exodus 15:26).

Respond

Think back through the past day and week and evaluate your attitude. Where would you fall on the grumble-meter if one is few grumble words and ten is many grumble words? What causes you to grumble? What might be the antidote for grumbling?

Prayer for the journey

Lord, guard my mouth from grumbling. Guard my heart from begrudging. Guard my soul from withering. Amen.

Waypoint 16

Daily watchamacallit

Read

> Then the LORD said to Moses, "Behold, I am about to rain bread from heaven for you, and the people shall go out and gather a day's portion every day, that I may test them, whether they will walk in my law or not." (Exodus 16:4)

Reflect

Above the dining table in my childhood home hung a print titled "Grace." The picture shows an elderly man bowing his head over a loaf of bread and a bowl of soup. It's from a photograph taken by Eric Enstrom of Bovey, Minnesota, during World War I for a photography convention. His goal was to communicate that even though people had to go without many things because of the war, they still had many reasons to give thanks.

My favorite part of the photo story is Enstrom's description of Charles Wilden, the peddler who became the subject of the photograph. "To bow his head in prayer seemed to be characteristic of the elderly visitor, for he struck the pose easily and naturally."[27] I recall the picture with fondness as it reminds me of God's faithfulness, not only to meet my daily physical needs, but also to meet my daily spiritual needs.

The Lord taught the Israelites on their journey. At this point in the expedition, they were getting hungry. In yet another miracle, God provided for them in an unprecedented way by presenting them with bread from heaven. They dubbed the strange substance "manna," which loosely translated is "whatchamacallit."[28] Each day they would rise and the manna would be waiting for them. They were to gather enough for that day and there was always enough for everyone. It was a daily reminder that God's presence was with them, as he provided sustaining mercy for them.[29]

Sister, God's sustaining mercy is there for you each day as well. The manna gathered by the Israelites is a spiritual metaphor for how God will feed you with his Word.[30] You need to gather your own "whatchamacallit" every day. You may not know how to expect God to work, but you can expect him to be faithful to meet the needs of the day. In the context of deployment, take a deployment one day at a time, and trust the Lord to provide grace for that day. I do not know about you, but I cannot make it by only going to church or chapel or a Bible study during the week. I need fresh nourishment each day.

Respond

"Give us this day our daily bread" (Matthew 6:11/Luke 11:3) is a prayer for God to provide spiritual nourishment for the unfolding day. How are you allowing him to do that for you? Can you remember a day when God provided just the right "whatchamacallit" for that day?

Prayer for the journey

Father, I pray you will nourish me with words of faith today. Give me what I need physically, mentally, emotionally, and spiritually to make it through this day. Thank you for your provision. Amen.

Waypoint 17

A plan for rest

Read

> And the LORD said to Moses, "How long will you refuse to keep my commandments and my laws? See! The LORD has given you the Sabbath; therefore on the sixth day he gives you bread for two days. Remain each of you in his place; let no one go out of his place on the seventh day. So the people rested on the seventh day. (Exodus 16:28–30)

Reflect

Among active-duty military spouses, a 2008 survey by the American Psychiatric Association found that 40 percent believed their husband or wife's service overseas hurt their own mental health. Approximately 25 percent reported regular problems with sleeplessness, anxiety, and depression.[31]

I found a note I wrote in my journal after spending some time with a group of deployed wives, "The moms with young kids seem worn out. Their kids are winning the battles. Lots of screaming, whining, one little guy was even growling. Lord, give these women the rest they need to face the days ahead."

Rest is an important and vital activity to God. Even he rested! "And on the seventh day God finished his work that he had done, and he rested on the seventh day from all his work that he had done" (Genesis 2:2).

Rest was important enough for God to build it into the schedule for the Israelites on their journey. On the sixth day of each week, God provided enough manna so they did not need to gather it on the Sabbath. This is the plan of a God who cares about his people getting needed rest.

God gave us the model to prepare ahead of time in order to take time to rest. I do not know about you, but the thing that most often robs me of rest is worry. Yet, I read about the provision God made for the Israelites and I ask how can I fret about the future when I know a God who makes such specific ahead-of-time plans?[32]

Respond

Quickly write a list of all the things that worry you and rob you of rest. Done? Okay, make that list your prayer list. Ask the Lord to work in each of those situations and to allow you to rest.

Prayer for the journey

Lord, "Lay your peace like a blanket over me and as I sleep I will rest in you." Amen. *(From "Tonight" by All Sons and Daughters)*

Waypoint 18

Grumbling—Second verse same as the first

Read

> But the people thirsted there for water, and the people grumbled against Moses and said, "Why did you bring us up out of Egypt to kill us and our children and our livestock with thirst?" So Moses cried to the LORD, "What shall I do with this people? They are almost ready to stone me." And the LORD said to Moses, "... Behold I will stand before you there on the rock at Horeb, and you shall strike the rock, and water shall come out of it and the people will drink." (Exodus 17:3–6a)

Reflect

Here it is again: grumbling. For the Israelites, it was not the first time and it certainly would not be the last. They sang another verse of "the grumbling in the desert song." In fact, grumbling became a recurring theme in their journey, like the song that never ends. Even with the miracles God did for them, they continued to question God's faithfulness.

God's response to the Israelites is astounding. God did not say, "I heard all this before, so I'm not listening again." No, he said, "I have heard this before and I see you are still struggling. Let me give you water out of a rock." He did not reward their grumbling, but he had compassion on them. He understood the exodus out of Egypt had turned their lives upside down and they were in new territory with many uncertainties and questions. God understood their human nature and his mercy prevailed.

On this side of history, it is easy to judge the Israelites until I hear myself singing the second verse of my grumbling song, which is the same as the first. You know what? God understands and his mercy prevails for me as well. Just because I experienced a victory over something last week does not mean I will experience that same victory this week. Israel grumbled because they did not see their problem of thirst as a spiritual problem. I grumble because I do not see many of my daily issues as spiritual problems.

In the book of Philippians, Paul addressed the issue of grumbling when he gave the instructions: "Do all things without grumbling or disputing" (Philippians 2:14). The phrase "all things" means just what it says.

Respond

The antidote for grumbling is gratitude. Take a few moments to list things or people for which you are grateful. Choose to sing a song of gratitude today.

Prayer for the journey

Today, use your gratitude list to offer thanksgiving to God.

Waypoint 19

Arm-in-arm

Read

> Whenever Moses held up his hand, Israel prevailed, and whenever he lowered his hand, Amalek prevailed. But Moses' hands grew weary, so they took a stone and put it under him, and he sat on it, while Aaron and Hur held up his hands, one on one side, and the other on the other side. So his hands were steady until the going down of the sun. And Joshua overwhelmed Amalek and his people with the sword. (Exodus 17:11–13)

Reflect

Last week, I had one of those "feeling overwhelmed by life" days. It felt like the world was on my shoulders and, like Moses, I felt that all would be lost if my bone-tired arms let down. Do you know such days? Your husband is the one deployed, but you are the one who is battle weary. When you are weary from sleeplessness, anxiety, responsibility, or just hard work, even the smallest thing can quickly escalate to feel like a major battle that could be lost at any moment.

In Exodus 17, the Israelites encountered a frightening threat. This time it was not food or water; it was a live and fully armed enemy. The Amalekites were a group of nomads that roamed the desert and harassed anyone who came near their turf. They were a tough and aggressive force.[33] The only way to defeat such an enemy was with the help of God. Moses standing on a hill as the mediator of God's divine power is quite a picture. When Moses raised his arms with his staff in hand, the Israelites were in control of the battle, but when Moses' arms were tired and started to drop, the Amalekites would gain momentum.

There was no magic in Moses' arms. Ultimately, the battle belonged to the Lord. He brought victory as Moses stood with arms outstretched. But God used others to give physical and spiritual help to Moses in the battle. Aaron and Hur gave *support,* a term meaning to strengthen somebody else.[34]

We need people who are strong when we are weak. When our personal endurance is in short supply, we need the help and support of others. May I tell you that it is okay to be weak sometime? Allow others to help you during times of weariness.

I am guilty of thinking I have to always be strong for others, that I have to do things for myself, that I must hide my insecurities. These things lead to isolation, loneliness, exhaustion, and defeat. As hard as it is, I am learning to be more vulnerable during my times of weakness. When I felt overwhelmed last week, I sent a text to a friend and asked for prayer. Just now, as I approached writing this waypoint, I received a text from her: "I am praying for you today. As you allow God to fill you with his strength, he will enable you for the moment. Just confront THIS moment with the resources he places in your hand."

My friend lives in another city. She does not know the details of my struggle. Yet, she held up my hands through prayer and words of encouragement.

Sister, who is holding up your arms today? Whose arms are you upholding?

Respond

How have you experienced help from friends during times of weakness? How can we provide such support for others?

Prayer for the journey

Lord, just as you were present to help the Israelites fight their battles, you are present to help me fight mine. Remind me that I do not have to fight alone. Make me willing to share my needs with others and help me be available to help others. Amen.

Waypoint 20

A little help

Read

> Moses' father-in-law said to him, "What you are doing is not good. You and the people with you will certainly wear yourselves out, for the thing is too heavy for you. You are not able to do it alone." (Exodus 18:17–18)

Reflect

If money were no object, which tasks would you hire out and which ones would you want to do yourself? Such a list will look different for each person. For most of us, money is a limited resource. However, the list you made can be a guide for where to look for a little help. Have you considered some creative ways to make that happen?

If you are a mom, you probably would enjoy having some help with your kids. Fortunately, there are positive activities for your kids such as the Awana youth program, a military chapel youth program like Club Beyond, scouting, youth center sports, and shared co-op childcare. Such activities can benefit your child, and create a little respite time for you. If the father-in-law of Moses were here, he would encourage you to take advantage of such things and enjoy a little time for yourself.

The military also offers assistance in other areas to include help with filing taxes, legal assistance, and career guidance. Counseling is available through military chaplains and Military OneSource. Honestly, there is no reason for you to go through a deployment depending only on your own resources.

We are all different in what we are able to handle, but we are all the same in our need to experience some margin and personal space. We need to take a lesson from Moses who thought it was easier to just do things alone. Yes, sometimes that is easier, but sometimes it is an excuse to try to stay in control of a situation.

The bottom line is if Moses—a called-by-God leader who God often filled with supernatural powers—needed some help, maybe you do too. Moses needed help when his personal resources were not enough to be effective. He needed a process to keep the work and responsibility from backing up and to avoid becoming inefficient. He stayed busy and always had something to do, but he was not doing it in the most efficient manner.

There are many tasks you must do, but you do not have to do everything yourself. Consider taking some time to tap into other resources and set priorities. Moses heeded his father-in-law's advice and started to take only the most important cases.

Respond

What resources are available to you during deployment? How are you using resources available to you?

Prayer for the journey

Lord, you never sleep, and you are always there for me. Help me be willing to ask for help, seek out help, and accept help during times when I feel overwhelmed. I cast all my anxiety on you because you care for me. Guide my steps today. Amen.

Waypoint 21

Need-to-know basis

Read

> They set out from Rephidim and came into the wilderness of Sinai, and they encamped in the wilderness. There Israel encamped before the mountain, while Moses went up to God. (Exodus 19:2–3a)

Reflect

I do not like people to keep me in the dark. I do not like people to keep me guessing. I do not like situations that are a need-to-know basis and someone has decided I do not need to know. What about you?

Unfortunately, deployment comes with the condition of information being disseminated on a need-to-know basis. As a deployed wife, I am not privy to discussions that directly affect my husband militarily. I cannot enter operation cells, step on a battlefield, and know details of location or mission. I may hear rumors, but until someone informs me through official channels, I am in the dark. Such situations force me to exercise trust in the military leadership.

The journey for the Israelites brought them to Mt. Sinai where Moses would meet God on behalf of the people. God did not allow the Israelites to go up the mountain and be a part of the conversation. They had to trust in Moses as their leader and believe that he would tell them what they needed to know. God kept even his select people in the dark regarding what was going on between him and Moses at that moment. Eventually, Moses informed the Israelites of all they needed to know about God and his grace.

The purpose of the Word of God is to teach us everything we need to know about God and his grace. Over thousands of years and by numerous authors of the Holy Scriptures, God revealed his plan of redemption through Jesus.

My sister, the plan of redemption is good news we all need to know. Praise God, he does not keep us in the dark!

Respond

What is your response to not knowing details about your husband's military situation? How can you be an agent of peace when others may be frustrated about such details?

Prayer for the journey

Lord, grant me peace when I am frustrated with unknowns. Help me to trust that you know the beginning from the end, and I can trust and not be afraid. Use me to bless others and allow me to be an agent of your peace today. Amen.

Waypoint 22

Truth in the midst of turmoil

Read

And God spoke all these words, saying . . . (Exodus 20:1).

Reflect

Rules, rules, and more rules. Just like some people see the military as only a life of rules and regulations, there are those who view the Ten Commandments as a list of rules impossible to keep and made to be broken. If this is your view, you miss a rich and endearing truth. The Ten Commandments are more than rules to live by; they are words that offer insight into the nature and character of a loving and just God.[35]

Do not miss the message held in Exodus 20:1: God himself uttered the words. He issued the commandments based on his personal and sovereign dealings with people whom he loved and who were to love and obey him.[36]

Thousands of years later, the public display of the Ten Commandments is an issue argued by lawyers in the highest courts of the land. Their mention brings contempt to some and comfort to others. The astonishing aspect of the Ten Commandments is that they were not carefully researched, debated, and organized by the wisest men in the best schools or seminaries of the day. As stated, God gave them in the midst of national turmoil for Israel. The Israelites left their homes, were chased by an army, lived day-to-day depending on food from heaven to survive, and never knew if the next place they moved to would have water. In essence, God turned their lives upside down and on the surface, their future looked uncertain. In the midst of this turmoil, God revealed divine truths that not only gave guidance then, but also have been words of truth for every generation since.

So what does that mean to a girl missing her husband? Challenging circumstances such as deployment can bring a feeling of turmoil. However, it may be during such a time that you find God come to you with a fresh understanding of his divine truth. Such truth can serve as a lasting guide not just for this deployment but also throughout your life. Look in God's Word; see what he has to show you.

It was during a deployment that Marie sought out a Bible study with some other women in her husband's unit. In Marie's own words:

> Reflecting back on four deployments, I can clearly see how God drew me closer to him during those times. This happened mostly through studying the Bible with other military wives. There, I found a safe place to explore God for who he is. God used his word and the relationships I developed in those studies to prune and grow me in my faith.

Respond

What are some things God is teaching you or has taught you during deployment? How have you made yourself open and available to learn things about God during this time?

Prayer for the journey

Lord, I pray for a teachable spirit. Help me to be open to the lessons and truths that will make a difference in the way I live my life today and in the future. Amen.

Waypoint 23

Tempted in the downtime

Read

> When the people saw that Moses delayed to come down from the mountain, the people gathered themselves together to Aaron and said to him, "Up, make us gods who shall go before us. As for this Moses, the man who brought us up out of the land of Egypt, we do not know what has become of him." (Exodus 32:1)

Reflect

When Glendon Perkins became a prisoner of war in North Vietnam, his wife Kay knew she would need strength to survive and to raise their four children. But she didn't know how much strength it would take. And she didn't know she would need it for six and a half years. "Now it seems like it was such a short time," Kay Perkins said. "While I was living through it, though, it seemed like an eternity."[37]

Kay Perkins waited for her husband to return from war for over six years. She was faithful. She was vigilant. She even found ways to help other wives who were waiting for their husbands to return. Glendon and Kay did not become a negative statistic of war.

The Israelites needed Kay Perkins around while they waited for Moses to return from atop the mountain. When Moses went on Operation Ten Commandments in the clouds with God, the Israelites down below did not know if he was just delayed or if he would even return at all. Moses was gone approximately six weeks when the Israelites became impatient. Their impatience implied that God had lost control of the situation.[38] Their faith in God was weak, so in the downtime they decided to take matters into their own hands. A later generation describes the scene in the Psalms: "But they soon forgot his works; they did not wait for his counsel. But they had a wanton craving in the wilderness, and put God to the test in the desert; ... They made a calf in Hebron and worshiped a metal image. They exchanged the glory of God for the image of an ox that eats grass." (Psalm 106:13–14, 19–20)

The Israelites went to Aaron and asked him to make a god they could see and touch. Aaron took their gold earrings and formed them into a golden calf. The guidelines for their new god allowed them to engage in immoral behavior. The situation that unfolded illustrates that when people give up on God, they turn to something else to satisfy their basic human nature.

Sister, guard your heart and mind in the downtime when mentally you know your husband will return, but emotionally it feels like it will never happen. Some have convinced themselves that adultery, substance abuse, or excessive shopping and eating can replace faithful waiting. Such activities only serve as an insufficient and superficial replacement for a close relationship with God that will enable you to wait faithfully.

Respond

What are some boundaries you can set for yourself in the downtime as you wait for your husband to return? What danger is there in dwelling on the thought that deployment is taking too long?

Prayer for the journey

Lord, it can be hard to wait. I grow impatient and restless and sometimes my imagination gets the best of me. Deepen my trust in you during times of waiting. Give me a calm assurance that your presence is with me and the waiting will soon be over. Amen.

Waypoint 24

Face-to-face

Read

> Thus the LORD used to speak to Moses face to face, as a man speaks to his friend. (Exodus 33:11a)

Reflect

If you could speak to your husband's commanding officer today, what would you say to him or her about your husband, yourself, and your family?

During this difficult time in the early years of the nation of Israel, Moses had the unique privilege of speaking face to face with God—as a man speaks to a friend. Moses was at home in God's presence.[39] There was unrestricted dialogue between Moses and God.[40] Moses spoke to God in a personal way about issues concerning the Israelites. He even spoke to God about his own personal struggles. This was a unique relationship. No other Israelites could speak with God in this way. The rest of the Israelites had to stand at the door of the tent. For them, God was at a distance.

Today, we have the privilege to have conversation with God in this same manner as Moses, based on the work of Jesus Christ and the presence of the Holy Spirit. Through the death and resurrection of Jesus, we have access to God the Father. We too may have unrestricted dialogue with God. The Holy Spirit helps us verbalize and communicate with God in ways we could not do on our own. The Holy Spirit knows the deep things in our heart that we may not even be able to verbalize. Romans 8:26 offers this description:

> Likewise the Spirit helps us in our weakness. For we do not know what to pray for as we ought, but the Spirit himself intercedes for us with groanings too deep for words (Romans 8:26).

Ultimately, that means our level of communication with God today can go beyond even the unique relationship God had with Moses!

The face-to-face discussions of Moses with God resulted in direction and renewed determination to lead. God filled Moses with the delight of his abiding presence.

So sister, pull up a chair, grab a cup of tea or coffee, and sit down with the Lord. Tell him the deep issues on your heart.

Respond

If you do not practice writing in a prayer journal, consider starting the practice. Such a journal can be a tool to facilitate spiritual growth and nurture your communication with God. How has prayer helped you through this deployment thus far? Using Scripture is an effective way to pray. Consider the prayer below taken directly from Paul's letter to the Romans.

Prayer for the journey

Father, help me in my weakness. I do not know what to pray as I ought. Thank you for your Spirit, who intercedes for me with groans too deep for words. Amen. (See Romans 8:26).

Waypoint 25

An answer vs. the answer

Read

> Moses said to the LORD, "See, you say to me, 'Bring up this people,' but you have not let me know whom you will send with me." (Exodus 33:12a)
>
> And [the LORD] said, "My presence will go with you, and I will give you rest." (Exodus 33:14)

Reflect

Wouldn't it be nice to have a step-by-step guide for navigating deployment? My guess is someone has attempted to write such a book, magazine article, or blog post. But who are they kidding? There are no formulas or systematic steps to make sure everything goes according to plan. Deployment is something you just have to go through. It reminds me of the children's verse about going on a bear hunt:

> *Can't go under it.*
> *Can't go over it.*
> *Can't go around it.*
> *Got to go through it.*

It is the *how* to go through a situation that can trip us on the way.

Moses found himself in need of direction on how to get through the desert and into the Promised Land. He came to God looking for an answer as if to say, "Show me the step-by-step way to get from here to there." He had a real need for God to give him practical guidance. Face it—this had not been an easy journey. The Israelites were a challenging group of people to lead and, besides, who knew what dangers they might encounter ahead.

At this point, God added a new dimension to the journey when he said to Moses, "My presence will go with you, and I will give you rest." Wow! In these few words God did not just provide *an* answer, God wanted Moses to see he was *the* answer.

God reassured Moses that he would bring the people through the desert to the Promised Land. He promised rest, which usually meant an end to evil, an enemy, hostility, or adversity.[41] More than that, God promised his very presence.

In the Gospel according to John, Jesus encountered a woman who was drawing water at a well (John 4:5–42). The woman was at the well for a practical reason—she needed water for her physical thirst. Jesus offered her living water. He did not just provide *an* answer; he wanted her to see he was *the* answer.

In the process of asking God how to get through a situation, do not miss the message that God wants not only to provide you practical help; he wants to provide you with his presence. Let God show you he *is* the answer you need.

Respond

Where do you fall on the *trust* versus *control* continuum? What makes it hard for you to trust God as *the* answer?

Prayer for the journey

Lord, forgive me when I grasp for control. Help me relinquish control to you as the answer to my every need. Amen.

Waypoint 26

Ten Commandments 'do-over'

Read

> And as soon as he came near the camp and saw the calf and the dancing, Moses' anger burned hot, and he threw the tablets out of his hands and broke them at the foot of the mountain. (Exodus 32:19)
>
> The LORD said to Moses, "Cut for yourself two tablets of stone like the first, and I will write on the tablets the words that were on the first tablets, which you broke." (Exodus 34:1)

Reflect

Doors slam. Fists pound. Hands slap. Voices rise. These are signs and symptoms of anger. Anger can cause an object, or even a relationship, to be smashed or destroyed. A popular blog site for military wives featured a post on "The Angry Stage of Deployment." The writer describes it this way:

> You know the time: probably at least a few months in, more likely somewhere past the halfway point, where your previously optimistic attitude deserts you and you are just mad. Mad at the military, mad at your spouse, mad at the whole situation.[42]

The comments generated from military spouses show how common an emotion anger is during deployment. The ever-present concern is not to do damage to anything or anyone in anger.

Moses was trusted with the Ten Commandments, written by the finger of God. What did Moses do in anger? He smashed the tablets! He was provoked by the sins the Israelites had committed in his absence. He could have put the tablets down and dealt with the sin calmly; but no, he got angry and smashed them. He destroyed what was holy, sacred, and given by God.

Sometimes we too succumb to the powerful emotion of anger. We smash precious relationships, throw down God-given parental oversight, or foolishly cause financial damage. Sometimes the damage can be overcome; but in other cases it is permanent. When the dust settles, what do you do with your broken tablets?

God says, "Cut out two more like the first." In his mercy and grace, God gives us a do-over and writes with his divine touch. God can make the second just as divine as the first. But a divine do-over is not without effort. God did not cut the stones. Moses had to cut them and carry them back up the mountain. God then used his divine finger to make them holy once more.

We do what God requires after we smash something in anger, but it is God's grace that allows us to be part of the do-over to restore and redeem what we damaged, or who we hurt.

Even though they were the Ten Commandments do-over, the words upon the stones still influenced not just Israel but the world from that day forward. What can God do with things you feel you have smashed? Do not limit God's transforming and redemptive grace. It is there especially for you.

Respond

How do you respond when you are angry? What does this passage teach you about dealing with anger?

Prayer for the journey

Thank you, Lord, for the promise of a do-over, the promise that you will redeem what I have damaged in my anger. Repair damage I have done to others, and help me to speak words of health and healing. Bring restoration and peace to my relationships and grant me the gifts of patience and kindness. Amen.

Waypoint 27

A look in the mirror

Read

> When Moses came down from Mount Sinai, with the two tablets of the testimony in his hand as he came down from the mountain, Moses did not know that the skin of his face shone because he had been talking with God. (Exodus 34:29)

Reflect

You know that awkward moment when you spot someone who used too much self-tanner. Their skin is an interesting orange hue that defies natural color. You do not want to stare, but cannot deny the shock of their abnormal appearance. I always wonder what such a person thinks when looking in a mirror.

On Mount Sinai, Moses had been with the Lord. Scripture says he did not know that the skin of his face shone. He could not see the change. He did not have a mirror. Moses only saw the shocked response of his audience to his bright and shining appearance.

This change of appearance occurred while, for the second time, Moses met with God and received the Ten Commandments. When he came back into public view, the people noticed a change.

The physical change in Moses' appearance from being in the presence of God is an illustration of how our spiritual countenance can appear different to others from our time spent communing with God. Moses did not try to fake the glow on his face. In fact, he did not know his face was shining. Unfortunately, there are people who act religious and righteous without the warmth of the glory of God glowing in their hearts. Sister, time in the presence of the Lord will make a difference in your life and your countenance.

You say, "But, I don't have that kind of time!" You may feel like you don't have hours to spend in prayer, but on the other hand how long does it take in the presence of Almighty God to make some change in your life? I believe that sometimes it only takes a moment. How long did it take the woman who touched the robe of Christ in the Gospel according to Mark (5:25–34)? In just a moment, she experienced a miraculous healing and transformation. A moment!

Am I suggesting that extended periods in Bible study and prayer is not necessary? No, that is not what I suggest. But, we cannot discount the impact of moments throughout the day when you hear a song that leads your heart to worship, or read a devotion or inspirational quote on your cell phone while waiting in line. There is no one formula for spiritual growth.

Respond

Read and meditate on these words from author Misha Boyett:

> "Enough time" is not a five-step plan, some secret sauce that nobody else has figured out. It's a spiritual condition of believing that there is enough time because God is enough, because God is making me enough. It's leaning into the reality of grace.

How can you lean into the reality of grace today?

Prayer for the journey

Father, make me fully present in this day. Help me be fully aware of your presence with me. Give me a countenance that shines with your glory! Amen.

Waypoint 28

You want us to build what?

Read

> [Moses said] "Let every skillful craftsman among you come and make all that the LORD has commanded." (Exodus 35:10)
>
> Then all the congregation of the people of Israel departed from the presence of Moses. And they came, everyone whose heart stirred him, and everyone whose spirit moved him, and brought the LORD's contribution to be used for the tent of meeting, and for all its service, and for the holy garments. (Exodus 35:20–21)

Reflect

Looking out my window the other day, I saw a building contractor accessing a lot across the street. That does not sound unusual—unless you saw the lot. It looks about as wide as a sidewalk. That is an exaggeration, but seriously, it is hard to believe someone is going to try to build a house on such an odd-shaped piece of land.

People build in strange places—just look at the Israelites in Exodus 35. They were getting ready for a major building project—in the middle of a desert! I have been through a major building project, and it was challenging even in the midst of a city where building materials were readily available. Through Moses, God tasked the Israelites to build a tabernacle in a place where they could not run to the local Desert Depot to pick up supplies they missed on the first run. Where would all the materials and qualified people come from in a wilderness?

If I were an Israelite during that time, I'm sure I would think of many reasons *not* to build while wandering in the desert. "Wouldn't it make more sense to wait until we arrive at the Promised Land? There, we will have an abundance of resources and skilled people. Think of the extra time we will have then, when picking up daily manna will not be on the agenda. Why build a tabernacle while on the move? That means we must move *it* wherever we go. Besides all of that, we are tired from traveling every day. Where will we find the energy to build such a monument?" Oh yeah, I could find plenty of excuses.

My summary of the situation would be: "We cannot do this now." Emphatically!

If you are like me, you can find plenty of excuses *not to do* something—not to build something—especially during a deployment.

Respond

What might the Lord be asking you to build during this time? Relationships? Memories? Organization? Health? What excuses might you be making in order not to build?

Prayer for the journey

Lord, I ask for courage, strength, and vision to build a godly life. Help me to embrace the tasks you have given me. Help me to hear your voice and your direction. Help me to willingly obey you and avoid excuses or distractions. Amen.

Waypoint 29

We did it!

Read

> This Moses did; according to all that the LORD commanded him, so he did. In the first month in the second year, on the first day of the month, the tabernacle was erected. (Exodus 40:16–17)

Reflect

There is nothing like the feeling that comes when you set and accomplish a goal.

You overcame the excuses. You set out to make something happen—and you did it!

I get that vibe when I read about the building of the tabernacle in Exodus. The account is a positive report of material, supplies, and labor offered freely by the Israelites to build something to honor God. It is amazing to account what was accomplished when everyone pooled their assets. There was more than enough material for the construction project. Those with specific talents completed their tasks and the result was intricate in detail and beautiful to behold. The people worked together. With God's direction and help, they built something incredible.

Scripture lists the amount of material used in construction as 2,400 pounds of gold, 8,400 pounds of silver, and 8,400 pounds of brass. Other materials included fabric, wood, and precious stones. In other words, the tabernacle ended up weighing a lot! It is difficult to comprehend that the Israelites carried this weighty edifice by hand, or even how, as they wandered for decades in the wilderness.

When it would have been easier to make excuses to build it, much less carry it on a journey, what motivated them to complete the task?

God revealed his name, his glory, and his presence to Israel at Mount Sinai. He wanted the Israelites to know he was not a *one place only* God. He was—is!—a *right in the middle of wherever you are* God. The tabernacle became the ongoing point of God's presence. It was the tangible reminder that God permanently dwelt among the Israelites, and it was a symbol of his promise to bless the nation.[43]

Respond

What reminds you of God's presence during this deployment? Where have you seen God right in the middle of a situation?

Prayer for the journey

Lord, I pray for daily reminders of your presence. Direct my thoughts to you throughout the day. Help me point others to you by my words and actions. Amen.

Waypoint 30

Dear Deployment

Read

So Moses finished the work. (Exodus 40:33b)

Reflect

We started this thirty-day journey with a letter from Tracie, a military wife who just completed the first month of a fourteen-month deployment. Here is her final letter to Deployment:

Dear Deployment,

Fourteen months is a long time—a lot of living happens, a lot of good days and bad, a lot of holidays and special occasions, a lot of the mundane and tedious, a lot of mistakes, and, praise Jesus—a lot of growth!

As we prepare to part ways (please don't take the huge smile on my face personally—it's not you, it's me), I want to thank you for being a tool in the hand of my God to change my family and me. We are not the same. Our family is more connected, and we have a stronger sense of purpose and direction than ever before. God used you to get us here—so, thank you! You have not been easy, but you have been worth it. You have been a trial (and that is putting it kindly), but you have also been a blessing, one for which I am truly grateful.

Over the past fourteen months, my family and I have experienced God's faithfulness and goodness. We have experienced the truth that God really does cause all things to work together for the good of those who love him and are called according to his purpose (Romans

8:28). We really can do all things through Christ who gives us strength (Philippians 4:13). God's presence has been with us and that has made all the difference.

With regards,
Tracie

P.S. Please do not mistake the thankful tone of my letter as an invitation to stay or as a welcome to return once you've left. While I sincerely appreciate the way God used you in our lives, I am very excited to say good-bye and I truly hope this is the last time we meet.

We could say of Tracie as Scripture says of Moses, she "finished the work." Tracie, and many women like her, have journeyed as if led by a pillar of cloud by day and a pillar of fire by night. They have questioned the direction of God's leading but have seen him be faithful to provide. They did not just take God along for the journey, or squeeze him in a suitcase as an afterthought. They followed where he led. God's presence in the midst of each day made all the difference.

Throughout the rest of this deployment, knowing God is with you will help you finish the journey and finish it well.

Respond

Take some time today to write your own letter to Deployment. Share your hopes, prayers, and desires for how you want to complete the journey.

Prayer for the journey

Lord, teach me to number my days that I may get a heart of wisdom. Satisfy me in the morning with your steadfast love so I may rejoice and be glad all my days. Let the favor of the Lord my God be upon me, and establish the work of my hands. Amen (from Moses' prayer in Psalm 90).

Journey 2

Reunited and Resilient

Introduction

Finally, your husband is home from deployment. Life can get back to normal. Right? But what is normal after experiencing deployment separation? How does a military family reintegrate?

Reintegration implies restoration—to return and fit back into position. Sounds simple enough, doesn't it? Yet a study of literature on reintegration yields a spectrum of information that highlights extremes of how to go about the process. You can find the simple lists of "do these five things and everything will be good" to "your soldier will return a completely different person plagued with PTSD." Both are a possibility, but in reality most military families fall somewhere in the middle of these extremes.

The buzzword for military families in recent years is resilience. Resilience is the ability to bounce back after challenging or traumatic circumstances. Resilient military families find ways to rebuild and repair the areas of a relationship that deployment may have weakened or damaged.

Scripture provides powerful examples of resilience through the lives of Ezra and Nehemiah. These men led redeployments of the nation of Israel after the nation experienced seventy years of captivity. God called them to aid in the reintegration of a people who endured the trauma of exile. They returned home and found buildings to repair and relationships to restore.

During this thirty-day journey of hope, we will travel with Ezra and Nehemiah as God used them to rebuild a sense of community and purpose to the nation. Their journey home included many things military families experience during the period of reintegration following a deployment.

As you go through each day's waypoint, don't forget to begin with the prayer from Psalm 119:18: Lord, "Open my eyes, that I may behold wondrous things out of your law."

Welcome to the journey!

Waypoint 1

God stirs a heart

Read

> In the first year of Cyrus king of Persia, that the word of the LORD by the mouth of Jeremiah might be fulfilled, the LORD stirred up the spirit of Cyrus king of Persia, so that he made a proclamation throughout all his kingdom and also put it in writing:
>
> "Thus says Cyrus king of Persia: The LORD, the God of heaven, has given me all the kingdoms of the earth, and he has charged me to build him a house at Jerusalem, which is in Judah. Whoever is among you of all his people, may his God be with him, and let him go up to Jerusalem, which is in Judah, and rebuild the house of the LORD, the God of Israel—he is the God who is in Jerusalem. And let each survivor, in whatever place he sojourns, be assisted by the men of his place with silver and gold, with goods and with beasts, besides freewill offerings for the house of God that is in Jerusalem." Then rose up the heads of the fathers' houses of Judah and Benjamin, and the priests and the Levites, everyone whose spirit God had stirred to go up to rebuild the house of the LORD that is in Jerusalem. (Ezra 1:1–5)

Reflect

I am a coffee snob. Some of you may roll your eyes, but others will recognize a kindred spirit. Maybe you can relate to some of my life mottos: "No coffee, no workee." Or, "I only need coffee on days ending with "y." And, "I would stop drinking coffee, but I am not a quitter." Each morning, I stir cream in my coffee—the real stuff. Do not give me a chemical facsimile. I will cut corners elsewhere, but for coffee I want *cream.* It is part of the morning ritual that awakens my senses and rouses me toward productivity.

Ezra 1:1 refers to God stirring a king to make a decision that would benefit God's people. The Hebrew word translated as *stir* is to rouse, awake, or incite.[1] God caused King Cyrus of Persia to fulfill a prophecy given by the prophet Jeremiah years earlier.[2] In Ezra 1:5, God stirred the hearts of families and priests to return to Jerusalem to rebuild the city. Yes, God awakened the senses of a king and a group of exiles to move toward rebuilding a nation.

Those who sensed God's stirring could have been content to have an emotional moment and go back to life as usual. However, just as stirring cream in my coffee each morning changes the color, texture, and taste, the stirring of the exiles brought change to their lives. The stirring moved them to find a new normal after being away from home for a very long time.

A major theme of the books of Ezra and Nehemiah is that God intervenes in our affairs by stirring hearts to action. He roused hope in the hearts of people long separated from their land, their temple, and their public worship. God stirred their hearts to work for the change and restoration they desired.

We may not understand wars and why they happen, but do not forget this: God is concerned about you and your military family. He can stir your family's hearts to reach for restoration as you journey toward reintegration following deployment.

Respond

How has God stirred you to prepare for reintegration? What comfort do you find in the fact that God stirred a king and influenced him to change the trajectory of a nation?

Prayer for the journey

Father, thank you for stirring hearts and for your intervention in people's hearts and lives. Help my family as we readjust to being together again. May we honor you in the process. Amen.

Waypoint 2

Recipients of god's care

Read

> And all who were about them aided them with vessels of silver, with gold, with goods, with beasts, and with costly wares, besides all that was freely offered." (Ezra 1:6)

Reflect

Last summer I had the privilege to meet and spend significant time with Brittany. Brittany, a Marine wife with three young and energetic children, draws you in with her infectious smile and positive disposition. She and her children received a scholarship for military families to attend a weeklong camp in the beautiful mountains of Colorado. Throughout the week, Brittany would stop and say, "I cannot believe I am here." She felt overwhelmed with the generosity of a Marine veterans' foundation that funded her entire trip. This group was willing to invest in a military family and pave the way for their reintegration following deployment.

Over the years, God has motivated many groups and organizations to action in order to help families in the process of redeployment. Oh, they may not recognize or acknowledge that it is God, but he is the originator of such good gifts. God is concerned about taking care of you. Just as God used people to aid in the restoration of the temple in the day of Ezra, he uses people today to aid in restoration of families.

The writer of Ezra emphasized the holy nature of the rebuilding. Neither a human plan nor project, the return and rebuilding was a work of God.[3] God moved on the hearts of Gentile people to give extravagant gifts and offerings toward the return of the Jews to their homeland. Such unexpected generosity could only be the result of God's intervention.

God can also awaken a desire for the restoration of relationships following such an event as military deployment. Brittany would tell you she was surprised and amazed to be the recipient of the generosity bestowed upon her. The gift came from an unlikely source of blessing, but such is often the case. God provides for those whom he loves—frequently in unexpected ways.

Respond

How has God provided for you in unexpected ways during deployment or reintegration? How have you been motivated to help others through deployment or reintegration?

Prayer for the journey

Lord, thank you for moving the hearts of people to do good in this world. Thank you for the times I have been a recipient of your care through the generosity of others. Challenge my heart toward love and good deeds today. Amen.

Waypoint 3

Family identity

Read

> Now these were the people of the province who came up out of the captivity of those exiles whom Nebuchadnezzar the king of Babylon had carried captive to Babylonia. They returned to Jerusalem and Judah each to his own town. (Ezra 2:1)

Reflect

Upstairs in my file cabinet sits a folder with several lists of names. One list holds the genealogy of my family and another list holds the genealogy of my husband's family. On the surface, you read a dry record of names. Most of the names mean very little to my husband and me, but they are representative of our family history. Our two narratives blend to become a story even more meaningful for our children. Within the list of names lies a secret to family resilience.

In a *New York Times* article entitled "The Stories that Bind Us," author Bruce Feiler asked, "What is the secret sauce that holds a family together? What are the ingredients that make some families effective, resilient, and happy?" Based on research Feiler concluded, "The single most important thing you can do for your family may be the simplest of all: develop a strong family narrative."[4]

The research reported by Feiler confirmed that the more children know about their family's history, the better able they are to deal with challenging situations. This confidence relates to a sense of belonging—of being part of a larger family. The research concludes that the sharing of stories about a family's positive moments, as well as, the ability to bounce back from difficult ones, increases the odds of a family thriving for generations to come.

On the surface, Chapter 2 of Ezra is a boring list of people long dead, but it represents so much more. The names listed are a record of God's faithfulness to his people. Hundreds of years of war, famine and captivity could not destroy the identity of God's people. God has preserved, is preserving, and will preserve his people.[5]

What are the stories of your family—both nuclear and extended—that you are telling? No matter the size of your family, you have a narrative that creates your family identity and will help carry you through difficult times.

Respond

What are ways you can preserve your family history? How have family stories helped you endure challenging times?

Prayer for the journey

Father, thank you for my family. Thank you for stories of faith, struggle, challenge, hope, and victory from which I learn in negative and positive ways. Help our family to be strong and bound together as we write the next chapter in our family story. Amen.

Waypoint 4

First, we worship!

Read

> When the seventh month came, and the children of Israel were in the towns, the people gathered as one man to Jerusalem. Then arose Jeshua the son of Jozadak, with his fellow priests, and Zerubbabel the son of Shealtiel with his kinsmen, and they built the altar of the God of Israel, to offer burnt offerings on it, as it is written in the Law of Moses the man of God. They set the altar in its place, for fear was on them because of the peoples of the lands, and they offered burnt offerings on it to the LORD, burnt offerings morning and evening. (Ezra 3:1–3)

Reflect

My vision blurred as I drove home from chapel on Sunday mornings during my husband's first deployment. The idea of eating lunch alone afterwards brought a flow of tears. Any other day of the week I was fine, but not on Sundays. I started to find excuses not to go to church in order to avoid the sad ride home following the benediction. Over time, I reached out to friends, and they reached out to me. Church no longer represented the loneliest day of the week, but instead became a place I corporately celebrated God's faithfulness.

Interesting enough, when my husband redeployed, church was one of the first places I wanted to go. I had sat through enough reintegration briefings to know we needed all the help we could get in order to reestablish our relationship.

I reminisced about that deployment as I read Ezra 3. Did you notice the first thing the Israelites did when they returned to Jerusalem was to build an altar to worship God? Such action speaks volumes about the foundation of their faith and their desire to reestablish worship as a priority for their nation.

The priests reconstructed the altar on the same foundation as the altar of Solomon's temple.[6] Do not miss the significance of this act. The rebuilding of the altar was the first step in setting apart the Jewish people as a nation once again.[7]

Scripture indicates that the people were fearful of the reconstruction because of opposition from the inhabitants of the land. But the altar represented God's protection and presence, which gave them more reason to be resilient in their effort to reconstruct.[8]

A 2011 study focused on challenges for military families during reintegration. Of crucial importance was a guiding belief system enabling a family to make sense of and find meaning in a difficult situation.[9]

Friend, keep worship a priority throughout the deployment and redeployment process. Consider church or military chapel to be one of the first places you go as a family. You might notify your pastor or chaplain about your husband's return and request recognition of the homecoming. What better way to mark a reunion than through worship in God's house?

Respond

Why might it be meaningful or significant for your church or chapel to recognize your reunion? Why do you think a "guiding belief system" is important to military families?

Prayer for the journey

Father, help me make worship of you a priority today and every day. May I continually offer up a sacrifice of praise to you, the fruit of my lips that acknowledge your name. Amen. (See Hebrews 13:5)

Waypoint 5

Stop and celebrate

Read

> And they sang responsively, praising and giving thanks to the LORD, "For he is good, for his steadfast love endures forever toward Israel." And all the people shouted with a great shout when they praised the LORD, because the foundation of the house of the LORD was laid." (Ezra 3:11)

Reflect

Military homecomings are often a remarkable sight. Flags, banners, yellow ribbons, a military band, and families with eager expressions all combine for a celebration getting ready to happen. As I type these words, I recall the anticipation I felt as I stood in a hanger and caught sight of a plane landing in the distance. I waited with other family members as the group of soldiers deplaned, lined in formation, and marched into the hanger. I craned my neck to find my soldier among the uniformed many and rejoiced when the formation dismissed. Then it came: shrieks and shouts, hugs and kisses, tears and laughter, and a massive rush to reunite with the one I missed for so long. Let the homecoming celebration begin!

Some of the same emotion of a military homecoming celebration is reflected in the words of Ezra 3:11. The difference lies in the timeline of the celebration. This celebration took place months after their reintegration back to Jerusalem, not at the point of their return. Although they had been home for some time, the people still faced months of work to fully reestablish the temple. Even so, they stopped and celebrated a major step – the foundation being laid – before they went any further.

As the Jewish people realized the significance of their progress, they began singing the same song used at the dedication of the first temple of Solomon's day.[10] Ecstatic, they gave a great shout in gratitude for what God had done, was doing, and would continue to do for their nation.[11] These people were ready to get on with God's plan, but first they stopped to celebrate a step in the right direction.

Sisters, reestablishing family norms after a deployment can take a long time. Take a lesson from the folks in Ezra and celebrate small accomplishments—even the first step toward the goal.

Respond

What is something you could do to mark and celebrate a step in the right direction after your husband returns from deployment? What positive results can come from such a celebration?

Prayer for the journey

Father, help our family to practice celebrating small steps in the right direction. Make us aware of the moments that may seem small, but are actually great strides forward. Give us creativity as we work together to build family memories. Amen.

Waypoint 6

The reintegration mash-up

Read

> But many of the priests and Levites and heads of fathers' houses, old men who had seen the first house, wept with a loud voice when they saw the foundation of this house being laid, though many shouted aloud for joy, so that the people could not distinguish the sound of the joyful shout from the sound of the people's weeping, for the people shouted with a great shout, and the sound was heard far away. (Ezra 3:12–13)

Reflect

Relieved because he is home, *but anxious for the adjustments we will have to make in the days ahead.*

Happy because he is part of the family again, *but sad for a loss of my personal independence.*

Excited because we can make plans, *but apprehensive for the emotional minefields through which we may have to walk.*

Peaceful because he is close, *but worried for the possibility of another deployment.*

Grateful because we can share responsibilities, *but frustrated to relinquish the way I have done things while he was away.*

Such is the *reintegration mash-up*. Pop culture defines a mash-up as a mixture or fusion of contrasting elements. Modern day singers have made the musical mash-up popular, but they do not have anything on the reintegration mash-up.

The contrasting emotions you may feel during reintegration are normal. In fact, you need to expect an emotional mash-up.

You cannot assume everything will be the same as it was before deployment. At the risk of sounding cliché, the best description is *finding a new normal.*

The returning Jews in the book of Ezra would have done well to know what to expect during reintegration. Notice the mixed emotions present in Ezra 3:12–13: Some shouted for joy, while others wept aloud. Notice too the reason for the weeping: things were not as they used to be. In remembering the temple before the exile, some focused on the negative which kept them from seeing the possibilities that change could bring.[12]

Sisters, heed this advice from experience: You gain nothing by saying, "I wish things were like they were before you deployed." Rejoice in the opportunity God has given you to be together again. Allow yourself permission to experience reintegration mash-up, but trust that God can help you navigate a good and blessed future.

Respond

In what ways have you experienced reintegration mash-up? How can you prepare yourself for or manage such conflicting emotions?

Prayer for the journey

Father, you created my emotions. I know I should not allow myself to be led by emotion more than I allow you to lead me. Help me not to live in the past or measure today by yesterday. Teach me to enjoy and appreciate today. Amen.

Waypoint 7

Discouragement: An enemy to defeat

Read

> Then the people of the land discouraged the people of Judah and made them afraid to build and bribed counselors against them to frustrate their purpose, all the days of Cyrus king of Persia, even until the reign of Darius king of Persia. And in the reign of Ahasuerus, in the beginning of his reign, they wrote an accusation against the inhabitants of Judah and Jerusalem." (Ezra 4:4–6)

Reflect

Have you met my enemy, Discouragement? This enemy likes to show up when progress is slow, preying on hopes, dreams, and goals. Seeping into a heart through a word, a look or a thought, it can sap your will to move forward. Determined and calculated, it sets out to defeat. It showed up in the Old Testament book of Ezra as the people of God demonstrated signs of progress. Trust me; it will make an appearance in your home as you and your husband work toward building togetherness following a deployment.

Discouragement will always be an uninvited caller. Any time you work to build something for God, you will encounter opposition. My friend, your marriage is something God wants to build. Marriage is to be an example of God and his church. As such, you better believe there is a big bulls-eye on the marriage relationship and Discouragement will zero in on the target. Be aware of attempts to hijack any success. Recognize the attack and expect it to show up—and then fight it with God's truth![13]

When fighting a battle, know your enemy. Discouragement is a tactic of the enemy of our soul, Satan. The word *accusation* used in Ezra 4:6 is translated from the Hebrew word *sitna,* a form of the word Satan, the adversary.[14] The New Testament book of Ephesians informs us that Satan is an *accuser* who uses schemes to discourage and hinder the good work God wants to do in our lives (Ephesians 6:11).

God does not leave us defenseless when we are attacked by Discouragement. He arms us with trust to cast all our cares on him (1 Peter 5:7) and confidence that God is working all things together for our good (Romans 8:28). Discouragement temporarily sidetracked the people of God until they refocused on what God wanted for them and then they went back to work. God wants good things for you and your marriage. Focus on what God is doing and Discouragement will retreat.

Respond

Fatigue, worry, lust, greed, selfishness, expectations. Circle the word or words that cause you to become discouraged. How can you apply the following Scripture to combat discouragement? "And let us not lose heart in doing good, for in due time we shall reap if we do not grow weary. So then, as we have opportunity, let us do good to everyone, and especially to those who are of the household of the faith" (Galatians 6:9–10).

Prayer for the journey

Father, sometimes I allow discouragement to get the best of me. Surrendering to discouragement is a choice I make when I focus on my circumstances. Help me see circumstances from your perspective. Increase my faith and let my focus be on you and what you want to do in my life. Amen.

Waypoint 8

One fell swoop

Read

> Therefore make a decree that these men be made to cease, and that this city be not rebuilt, until a decree is made by me. (Ezra 4:21)

Reflect

After my husband's first deployment, I had the idea that once he was home, everything would go back to business as usual. I expected him to bare his soul and tell me all about the experience. We would rid ourselves of any negative issues at the start, be on the same page, and finally move on from the months-long intrusion into our lives. In my naiveté I planned to deal with reintegration in one fell swoop.

Yes, my plan was naïve, but I did not know any better. After that initial slow-motion movie moment of reunion, when we put away the flags and yellow ribbons, we met with opposition in our communication, intimacy, finances and overall re-sorting of roles. Reintegration was going to take longer than I expected, and my timetable went through a major adjustment.

My friend, Susan, has experienced more deployments than she can count. She believes reintegration is too broad a topic to label as one big task to do. She wisely refers to reintegration as many pieces in a process we must go through. The timetable for the pieces cannot be set, and will be different for the spouse as well as any children in the family.

Knowing their purpose as a nation was to reestablish worship, rebuild the temple, and reaffirm their relationship with God, the Jews in the Old Testament book of Ezra returned to their homeland. Their call was sure. Their goal was righteous. Their timetable was set. However, they did not execute the mission as simply and quickly as they thought they would. Instead of one quick action of building, issues caused the process to take longer than expected. The opposition that formed against them forced an adjustment to their timetable.

Eventually, the Jews resumed building and the work was completed. No doubt, some returning exiles abandoned hope and walked away from the rebuilding. For the discouraged, the opposition proved too great, the waiting too long and the process too hard.

God is all about completing work he starts. The New Testament book of Philippians confirms this promise, "And I am sure of this, that he who began a good work in you will bring it to completion at the day of Jesus Christ" (Philippians 1:6). Guard yourself from approaching reintegration after redeployment as a project; rather treat it as a process. Reintegration with your spouse is not something you will need to complete before you move on to other marriage issues. Progress in the process should be our goal.

Respond

What are some areas of progress you see in your marriage relationship during reintegration? What are areas in which you would like to see progress?

Prayer for the journey

Father, thank you for the work you started in me. Thank you for the work you started in my marriage. Help me to trust you in the process of making progress toward loving and God- honoring relationships. Amen.

Waypoint 9

The hand of God

Read

> Blessed be the LORD, the God of our fathers, who put such a thing as this into the heart of the king, to beautify the house of the LORD that is in Jerusalem, and who extended to me his steadfast love before the king and his counselors, and before all the king's mighty officers. I took courage for the hand of the LORD my God was on me, and I gathered leading men from Israel to go up with me. (Ezra 7:27–28)

Reflect

Fast-forward through several chapters in the book of Ezra and we come to a second redeployment. Chapter 7 finally introduces us to the namesake of this Old Testament book. A scribe, Ezra was a religious man given the job of interpreting the law of God for the Jewish community.[15] The Babylonian king gave Ezra the mission to redeploy to Jerusalem with valuable supplies, funds and a fresh group of returning exiles.

Ezra's words here in chapter 7 provide a key to the success of his redeployment: he recognized the hand of God in his situation. Ezra was not a free man in the sense that he could go where he wanted to go, when he wanted to go. (No, he was not in the military!) He was an exile banished from his homeland working for a foreign king. Yet, in that place he chose not to be a victim of his circumstance. As he reflected, he took courage in the many ways God's hand had been, and therefore would be, upon him.

What does it mean for the hand of God to be upon you? It means the blessing, help, strength and power of God are working on your behalf. What was it about Ezra that made the hand of God so evident in his life and work? The key is found in Ezra 7:9–10: "For on the first day of the first month he began to go up from Babylonia, and on the first day of the fifth month he came to Jerusalem, for the good hand of his God was on him. For Ezra had set his heart to study the Law of the LORD, and to do it and to teach his statutes and rules in Israel."

Ezra set his heart to learn what God wanted him to learn, to apply what he learned to his situation, and to then share what he learned with others. Even though the Word of God that guided Ezra was written hundreds of years before he was born, he recognized the truths were relevant for his day. The Bible we have today, though it has been around for a long time, is still relevant. God honors his Word. We can better see his hand on our lives when we have his Word in our hearts.

Respond

Read chapters 7 and 8 of the book of Ezra and underline each reference to *the hand of God*. What do you learn about God's blessing through these passages? How can you apply what you read to resilience and reintegration?

Prayer for the journey

Father, thank you for your hand that offers me help, protection, comfort, provision and guidance. Help me not to forget your hand rests upon me as I journey through this day. Amen.

Waypoint 10

Fragile—handle with care!

Read

> I gathered them to the river that runs to Ahava, and there we camped three days. (Ezra 8:15a)
>
> Then I proclaimed a fast there, at the river Ahava, that we might humble ourselves before our God, to seek from him a safe journey for ourselves, our children, and all our goods. (Ezra 8:21)

Reflect

After my husband returned home from one deployment, I spent days wanting to wear a sign around my neck: FRAGILE—Handle with Care! The feeling of fragility was real and brought along its friend, *fear*. I wondered if we would reach the destination—integration as a family unit. I wondered if I had what it took.

During my husband's absence, I attended to the needs of other deployed spouses. My kids were in a new season that required less physical, but more emotional, energy. My position as a leader for a military ministry involved an intense travel schedule. I was tired—no, I was beyond tired; I was weary. A good friend and fellow military wife suggested that many spouses experience a form of "compassion fatigue" following repeated deployments. Between taking care of other military families and trying to take care of your own family, the impact can be debilitating. Compassion fatigue is cumulative and residual. After caring for others during trauma, we can experience fragility.

Ezra demonstrated principles applicable to a weary military spouse who feels she does not have what she needs for a successful reintegration journey. It is clear in Ezra 8 that Ezra felt fragile. He faced a 900-mile journey on a camel and did not have the people to guard the vast treasure he had to transport. He planned to move articles from the temple, and the Jewish law put Levites in charge of such articles. Ezra searched the camp and found no Levites. He felt responsible for both people and goods. He wanted to make this journey with God's blessing.

What did he do when he was not sure how to move forward? *He stopped and prayed.* I am not offering a flippant "Just pray about it." What we see in Ezra is a model of what to do when faced with a faith-testing circumstance. When he felt weak in his situation, he leaned even more into God's provision. Praying and fasting was not only a way to ask for God's help, it was also an acknowledgement of his inability to go in his own strength. If attacked by robbers along the journey, he knew he had no armed guards to protect his traveling band. He humbled himself before God, and the Lord answered his prayer by providing safe passage to Ezra and the other defenseless travelers (Ezra 8:31–32).

The apostle Peter endorsed this example centuries later when he wrote, "Humble yourselves, therefore, under the mighty hand of God so that at the proper time he may exalt you, casting all your anxieties on him, because he cares for you" (1 Peter 5:6–7). Our good and faithful God will help you in times of weariness and fragility. He never tires or becomes weary in his compassion for you. He can help you arrive at your destination refreshed, renewed, and *reintegrated.*

Respond

What do you learn about God from Lamentations 3:22–24 and Isaiah 40:28? When you are tired and weary, how does it help to know God does not grow tired or weary?

Prayer for the journey

Lord, thank you for your steadfast love. May your love embrace me, your mercy protect me, and your faithfulness sustain me. Amen.

Waypoint 11

Financial planning

Read

> I weighed out into their hand 650 talents of silver, and silver vessels worth 200 talents and 100 talents of gold, 20 bowls of gold worth 1,000 darics, and two vessels of fine bright bronze as precious as gold. And I said to them, "You are holy to the LORD, and the vessels are holy, and the silver and the gold are a freewill offering to the LORD, the God of your fathers. Guard them and keep them until you weigh them before the chief priests and the Levites and the heads of fathers' houses in Israel at Jerusalem, within the chambers of the house of the Lord." (Ezra 8:26–29)
>
> We came to Jerusalem, and there we remained three days. On the fourth day, within the house of our God, the silver and the gold and the vessels were weighed into the hands of Meremoth the priest, son of Uriah, and with him was Eleazar the son of Phinehas, and with them were the Levites, Jozabad the son of Jeshua and Noadiah the son of Binnui. The whole was counted and weighed, and the weight of everything was recorded. (Ezra 8:32–34)

Reflect

In her article "Seven Things I Wish I'd Known about Military Marriage," military wife Jacey Eckhart topped the list with, "I wish I paid a whole lot more attention to money."[16] Couples often do not realize the role money plays in a relationship. The way we spend and account for money can be how we spell TRUST.

Jokes about "retail therapy" can bring a smile, but the result of emotional spending can be anything but funny. Budgeting for an occasional splurge is fun and, I would argue, even healthy. But when spending money becomes a necessary part of celebrating or forgetting the highs and lows of life, a flag should go up.

"Arguments about money are by far the top predictor of divorce. It's not children, sex, in-laws, or anything else. It's money—for both men and women." This statement from researcher Sonya Britt gives insight into why finances are a topic included in official deployment and redeployment briefings. Another study, "Examining the Relationship between Financial Issues and Divorce", substantiates Britt's statement. That research also confirms that arguments about money tend to be more intense and last longer than other types of marital disagreements.[17]

Ezra offers a practical lesson on money management for married couples. Notice in chapter 8 of Ezra, before he set out to return home and after he arrived home, he directed the travelers to do an accounting of their financial assets. The plan to rebuild the temple would carry with it a cost, and Ezra was careful to guard the funds entrusted to him.

Dear one, do not discount the importance of making a financial plan for your marriage, especially during deployment. Rebuilding always has a cost, whether monetary or emotional. The attitude you and your husband have toward money can be the key to a successful and peaceful reintegration.

Respond

What have you and your husband done to navigate the financial issues of marriage? What can you do to ensure financial success as you look toward reintegration?

Prayer for the journey

Father, help me to do my part in making my marriage financially sound. Give us wisdom in how we manage our finances and help us to be in unity in the method. Amen.

Waypoint 12

Solidarity and support

Read

> As soon as I heard this, I tore my garment and my cloak and pulled hair from my head and beard and sat appalled. Then all who trembled at the words of the God of Israel, because of the faithlessness of the returned exiles, gathered around me while I sat appalled until the evening sacrifice. (Ezra 9:3–4)

Reflect

Whoa! Tearing of garments … pulling hair from head and beard … such strange behavior! What happened to cause this reaction? First, Ezra's strange behavior was typical of ritual mourning in response to extreme crisis.[18] What was the crisis? A group of concerned leaders reported the gross misconduct that was taking place in the Jewish community. You see, the Jews were to be a separate people, but they had mixed themselves with pagans. The crisis was not about ethnicity or race, but worship and holiness. The disobedience of God's people was devastating to Ezra. He sat appalled in seemingly helpless frustration.[19]

Let's get back to the strange behavior. In the Near Eastern culture of Ezra's day, expressing anguish in an overt and public manner was acceptable. Ezra's actions communicated the intense emotion and profound sorrow he felt for the condition of his community. Such behavior today would be cause for alarm and reason for a 911 call. Ezra's unusual exhibition brought into the open the misconduct issue. The people became aware of the situation and gathered in solidarity around Ezra.[20]

I wish we still practiced grief rituals that would rid oneself of such conflict and alert others of the need for solidarity. Perhaps such cultural rituals to deal with traumatic experiences and loss would be beneficial.

Today, in the context of military personnel returning from battle, strange behavior may be an indication of internal conflict. As a spouse, you can be watchful for signs of behavior that alert you to a need for help. Within three months of deployment, is anything preventing your military man from returning to a full and normal life?[21]

Your initial response should not be to criticize your military man and insist he change his new and unacceptable behavior. Keep in mind these actions may be a result of unseen internal conflict. Talk to a trusted professional like a military chaplain if you are not sure how to approach your husband. Chaplains can confidentially give insight into what your husband's strange behavior means and recommend a solution. You may learn that uncommon behavior by returning troops is very common. Such behavior can indicate a need for help in the readjustment process.

Respond

Whom can you intercede in prayer for today? List their names in a journal or on a paper to keep in your handout. Take the time to let them know you are standing with them in solidarity.

Prayer for the journey

Father, today I lift ________________________ to you. I ask you to help them in their time of trouble. Be their strength, their hope and their deliverer. Show me how I can be a practical help to them in their time of need. Amen.

Waypoint 13

How's your posture?

Read

> And at the evening sacrifice, I rose from my fasting, with my garment and my cloak torn, and fell upon my knees and spread out my hands to the LORD my God. (Ezra 9:5)

Reflect

Do you recall the posture of Ezra in yesterday's reading? I do, because it is a posture in which I can be stuck. Ezra said, "*I sat appalled.*" Other translations of the word *appalled* include overcome, devastated, or stunned. Bad news, unmet expectations, or disappointing results can paralyze me and I can sit appalled, devastated, stunned, overcome.

The example of Ezra here in Ezra 9:5 provides a model for emotionally paralyzing situations. We see that Ezra allowed himself to feel all the negative emotions that came with bad news, but he did not stay in that dark place. At a set time, he rose and took his emotions to God in prayer. Ezra knelt, bowed his head, and spread out his hands to plead with God for help. His posture communicated need, humility, and submission to God.[22] His position changed from one of sitting on his hands feeling hopeless, to one of falling on his knees feeling hopeful.

Whether it is bad news, or inner struggles, the temptation to sit appalled is real.

What posture do you take when you are discouraged, hear bad news, or are having a bad day? You may sit like Ezra, drape yourself across your bed, or curl up in a fetal position. The posture is only the indicator of the position of your heart. A change in heart normally presents a change in posture.

Look at yourself in the proverbial mirror. When you are in your "appalled" posture, follow the example of Ezra. Allow yourself some time to sit there, take note of the emotions that simmer in this posture, and then make the determination—and it may take all your strength—to stand up. Stand up spiritually in prayer. In making the change to a positive posture, you will begin to see progress.

Respond

What is your emotional posture today? Taking note of your emotions, how will you make the determination to stand?

Prayer for the journey

You, O Lord, are a shield about me, my glory, and the lifter of my head (Psalm 3:3). Amen.

Waypoint 14

Confession

Read

> [Ezra said] "O my God, I am ashamed and blush to lift my face to you, my God, for our iniquities have risen higher than our heads, and our guilt has mounted up to the heavens. From the days of our fathers to this day we have been in great guilt. And for our iniquities we, our kings, and our priests have been given into the hand of the kings of the lands, to the sword, to captivity, to plundering, and to utter shame, as it is today. (Ezra 9:6–7)

Reflect

To review: The Jewish people married those who were members of ungodly, pagan religions. Jewish law prohibited this practice. The disobedience of the people broke Ezra's heart and he felt the need to confess to God for the sin of the people. You can read the prayer of Ezra in its entirety in Ezra 9:5–15. The moving prayer expresses immense guilt. How much guilt, you ask? Enough to be *"mounted up to the heavens."* What a lot of guilt! The Jews consistently tested God's goodness, compounding their long-standing pattern of guilt.

In my mind, I see Ezra with hair wild and clothes torn. In the dirt, on his knees, his hands outstretched, he looks up to heaven. On his face is an earnest and intense expression. As he pleads with God, the waves of grief for the past sins of his people multiply—wave upon wave—he confesses the cumulative effect of disobedience. The wrongs have mounted over time to create a great burden.[23]

Guilt is a heavy burden and it can weigh down your soul. *Confession* is a heavy action, but it can relieve a weighty burden.

Reintegration following a deployment may drudge up guilt that can cover a wide spectrum of thoughts and deeds. On one end of the spectrum can be negative words or attitudes that you and your spouse need to confess to the Lord and to each other. On the other end of the spectrum can be things that are not as easy to put behind you. A word of caution: be careful about making confession directly to your spouse. Sometimes this can do more harm than good. Some Christian denominations practice formal confession, while others encourage talking with a trusted counselor or chaplain.

If you feel the need to confess, do not ignore the need, but do it responsibly. Just as God heard Ezra's prayer of confession, we all can find hope in the promise stated in 1 John 1:9, "If we confess our sins, he is faithful and just to forgive us our sins and to cleanse us from all unrighteousness."

Respond

What do you learn about confession from Ezra's prayer in Ezra 9:6–15? Spend time asking the Lord to reveal anything in your own life about which you need to mourn and for which you need to confess.

Prayer for the journey

Lord, I acknowledge my sin to you and do not cover my iniquity; I will confess my transgressions to you and you will forgive the iniquity of my sin. You are a hiding place for me; you preserve me from trouble; you surround me with shouts of deliverance. Amen. (See Psalm 32:5, 7)

Waypoint 15

A brief moment

Read

> "But now for a brief moment favor has been shown by the LORD our God, to leave us a remnant and to give us a secure hold within his holy place, that our God may brighten our eyes and grant us a little reviving in our slavery. For we are slaves. Yet our God has not forsaken us in our slavery, but has extended to us his steadfast love before the kings of Persia, to grant us some reviving to set up the house of our God, to repair its ruins, and to give us protection in Judea and Jerusalem." (Ezra 9:8–9)

Reflect

Do you think we remember life by significant moments? The ordinary passes as a blur, but then comes *a moment* when something happens that changes the trajectory of a day, a year, or a lifetime. A moment is brief, but it can be historic.

The opening words of Ezra 9:8 indicate the significance that can come in a brief moment. As Ezra prayed, he compared the power of one brief moment of God's favor in contrast to the many years the Jews walked in disobedience. He recognized and acknowledged God's grace at work enabling them to survive and return to their homeland.

Read Ezra 9:8–9. Packed into a few words you will see a lot of grace shown to the Jewish people. That grace secured their future (*given a secure hold*), encouraged their hearts (*brighten our eyes*), extended their hope (*grant us a little reviving*), renewed their purpose (*set up the house of God*), and promised their protection (*to give us protection in Judea and Jerusalem*).[24]

These folks had been in exile so long that they seem to have suffered some disorientation. They struggled to reconcile their identity from before the exile with their identity now that they have returned home. In Ezra's prayer of confession, he connected the past to the present. He did not sugarcoat the struggles of the past, but reminded the people that God was with them even in the difficult times. Now, God is still with them to offer fresh courage to do the work of rebuilding the temple and restore worship to their God.[25]

Dear sister, do not discount the significance of a moment. The process of reintegration takes place moment by moment. Give the Lord the moments of your day and trust him to be your security, your hope, your purpose, and your protection.

Respond

Ezra 9:8–9 is a picture of God going the extra mile on behalf of the Jewish people. How have you seen God go the extra mile for you? What fresh courage is the Lord giving you for the work ahead?

Prayer for the journey

Father, thank you for moments of grace that you have bestowed throughout my life. I never want to squander your grace or be unappreciative of your goodness. May I accept it all with gratitude. Amen.

Waypoint 16

'We need to talk'

Read

> The words of Nehemiah the son of Hacaliah. Now it happened in the month of Chislev, in the twentieth year, as I was in Susa the citadel, that Hanani, one of my brothers, came with certain men from Judah. And I asked them concerning the Jews who escaped, who had survived the exile, and concerning Jerusalem. And they said to me, "The remnant there in the province who had survived the exile is in great trouble and shame. The wall of Jerusalem is broken down, and its gates are destroyed by fire." As soon as I heard these words I sat down and wept and mourned for days, and I continued fasting and praying before the God of heaven. (Nehemiah 1:1–4)

Reflect

"We need to talk." No one would argue that communication is a key ingredient to a healthy marriage, but prefacing a conversation with these four words can cause dread in the most talkative spouse. Effective communication is not an innate skill, but something we must learn. Research verifies the importance of communication in building and maintaining marriage relationships. Research has also shown that reestablishing communication is one of the challenging hurdles couples must face during reintegration and post-deployment.[26]

Just consider the on-going practice of OPSEC (Mission Operational Security) during a deployment. As a couple, you may have communicated regularly via text, email, or video-chat, but there were things your military husband could not discuss. Moreover, you may have kept some information from your husband that you did not want to worry him about during his deployment. If not addressed, these protective practices could become a pattern of keeping secrets after reunion.

Nehemiah 1 offers an example of healthy communication. Some Jewish leaders came to Nehemiah and said, "We need to talk." They gave an assessment of what was going on in Jerusalem. The need for repair and restoration was significant both for the people and for the city. Nehemiah listened with empathy to their assessment about the city. Honest communication motivated him to set a goal to improve the situation.

Communication is necessary to evaluate your circumstances following a deployment. Guard yourself from glossing over reality and succumbing to the "I'm fine ... Everything is fine ..." defense. Communicate with your spouse. Give each other space to offer an assessment of how things have been and express what needs to happen to rebuild your family. Ask God to give you an empathetic heart to understand your spouse's needs.

Nehemiah also went to the Lord and said, "We need to talk." The pain the remnant experienced moved him to pray and fast on their behalf. The issues caused him personal pain, but he did not focus on himself and the effect the news had on him.

Be assured you too can come to the Lord and say, "We need to talk." God is ready and willing to listen.

Respond

In what ways have you become more aware of your spouse's needs since deployment and reintegration? Has communication with your spouse become better or worse since deployment or reintegration? How have you seen this demonstrated?

Prayer for the journey

Father, I pray today for improved communication between my husband and me. Teach us to listen to one another—to be slow to speak and quick to hear. Amen. (See James 1:19)

Waypoint 17

'What's wrong?'

Read

> In the month of Nisan, in the twentieth year of King Artaxerxes, when wine was before him, I took up the wine and gave it to the king. Now I had not been sad in his presence. And the king said to me, "Why is your face sad, seeing you are not sick? This is nothing but sadness of the heart." Then I was very much afraid. I said to the king, "Let the king live forever! Why should not my face be sad, when the city, the place of my fathers' graves, lies in ruins, and its gates have been destroyed by fire?" Then the king said to me, "What are you requesting?" So I prayed to the God of heaven. And I said to the king, "If it pleases the king, and if your servant has found favor in your sight, that you send me to Judah, to the city of my fathers' graves, that I may rebuild it." (Nehemiah 2:1–5).

Reflect

Hiding some of your feelings and concerns is easy when you are thousands of miles away from your spouse. Even if your communication was steady during deployment, having your military man at home can be up close and personal. For some, "up close and personal" can translate to "in my space and awkward."

Nehemiah's job description was cupbearer to the king. Persian kings were famous for their drinking parties. The cupbearer was the designated person to carry the wine and give it to the king. Chapter 2 of Nehemiah takes place about four months after Nehemiah received the bad news about the poor condition of Jerusalem. As Nehemiah handed a cup of wine to the king, the king noticed Nehemiah's sad countenance. Not wanting gloominess to overcome his party and showing some genuine concern, he asked Nehemiah the reason for his sad face.

How do you generally respond when someone asks, "What's wrong?" You may really want to tell them, but at the same time, you are terrified of the reaction. What if they minimize your feelings or doubt your reasoning? What if you have been working up the courage to ask a question and finally the opportunity comes, but you are suddenly afraid of the possible answer?

Perhaps such thoughts were swirling in the mind of Nehemiah when the king asked him, "What's wrong?" Was the king angry because he was sad during a festive moment? Would the king react favorably to Nehemiah's concern for Jerusalem?

We are not privy to why Nehemiah became afraid, but what stands out to me is that he overcame his fear. He asked the king to let him go to rebuild Jerusalem.

When you are face to face with your spouse, you can read in his countenance what you may never see in a text message or email. It takes concern to ask, "What's wrong?" It takes courage to open up and share what is bothering you. Love shows concern and is courageous. Love overlooks imperfections for criticism, but searches out hurts for healing. Some people are more intuitive than others. Do your best to listen carefully for pain within your spouse. If you think you hear it, ask the question. Take time to understand your spouse's pain and ask the Lord's help for healing.

Respond

What does Psalm 42:5 tell you about countenances? What would you answer if God asked you, today, "What's wrong?"

Prayer for the journey

Father, thank you for being *a shield about me, my glory, and the lifter of my head* (Psalm 3:3). Help me to be honest with my words and caring with my actions. Amen.

Waypoint 18

The fine art of discretion

Read

> So I went to Jerusalem and was there three days. Then I arose in the night, I and a few men with me. And I told no one what my God had put into my heart to do for Jerusalem. There was no animal with me but the one on which I rode. I went out by night by the Valley Gate to the Dragon Spring and to the Dung Gate, and I inspected the walls of Jerusalem that were broken down and its gates that had been destroyed by fire. Then I went on to the Fountain Gate and to the King's Pool, but there was no room for the animal that was under me to pass. Then I went up in the night by the valley and inspected the wall, and I turned back and entered by the Valley Gate, and so returned. And the officials did not know where I had gone or what I was doing, and I had not yet told the Jews, the priests, the nobles, the officials, and the rest who were to do the work. (Nehemiah 2:11–16)

Reflect

We live in a TMI culture—too much information. People process the deep dark things of life on social media for the entire world to read. Am I the only one who struggles with such blatant openness? I will just say it: Some folks need to rediscover the fine art of discretion. I know, I know—I am on a soapbox and sound preachy. Forgive me. No, I take that back. I believe there *is* some information you need to keep to yourself.

I admire Nehemiah's discretion. He arrived in Jerusalem knowing the task to rebuild was not going to be easy. We find out right away that he encountered folks who were not happy about his presence and his purpose (Nehemiah 2:9–10). He did not overreact to the criticism, nor did he rush to pull together supporters to start an immediate building project. The journey had been long, and the task ahead would take energy, so he rested.

After resting for three days, he still did not rally the people to action. Instead, he went out at night when no one else was around. He surveyed the ruins and quietly processed his thoughts. He made an honest assessment to create a practical plan. Too much was at stake to rush. He needed firsthand knowledge.[27] Nehemiah knew he could not do the work of rebuilding alone, but he needed to spend time alone to understand his role.

When I feel needy or frustrated, my first tendency is to run to anyone who will listen. Social media adds a new dimension to "anyone." When seeking help for your family in time of frustration or crisis, be intentional about the whom and where. Too much personal information on social media can become embarrassing, even harmful. There are good places to go for help. Go to specific, confidential people to process. Learn a lesson in wisdom from Nehemiah, and put some time and space between stimulus and response.

Respond

When you come into a new situation, like the one awaiting Nehemiah in Jerusalem, do you tend to:

a) Complain about the work ahead?
b) Run to anyone who will listen?
c) Go straight to work?
d) Assess the situation first?

What positive strategies can you follow when dealing with social media and personal issues?

Prayer for the journey

Lord, give me patience to listen and wait before I speak and act. Give me your wisdom to navigate life and relationships. Amen.

Waypoint 19

Own the vision

Read

Then I said to them, "You see the trouble we are in, how Jerusalem lies in ruins with its gates burned. Come, let us build the wall of Jerusalem, that we may no longer suffer derision." And I told them of the hand of my God that had been upon me for good, and also of the words that the king had spoken to me. And they said, "Let us rise up and build." So they strengthened their hands for the good work. But when Sanballat the Horonite and Tobiah the Ammonite servant and Geshem the Arab heard of it, they jeered at us and despised us and said, "What is this thing that you are doing? Are you rebelling against the king?" Then I replied to them, "The God of heaven will make us prosper, and we his servants will arise and build, but you have no portion or right or claim in Jerusalem." (Nehemiah 2:17–20)

Reflect

Time and distance have a way of making even the strongest of relationships feel vulnerable. No matter how hard you have tried to stay connected, cracks in the wall will need repair. Time and distance also have a way of making the cracks in a relationship appear wider and impossible to mend. Do not believe such things. Hard to repair? Yes. Impossible to mend? No.

When Nehemiah inspected the wall, he discovered for himself that the walls were in ruins. After looking at the mess, Nehemiah said, "You see the trouble we are in . . ." The Hebrew word for *trouble* used here is a very strong word communicating that evil could come upon them because of the defenseless condition of their city.[28] Nehemiah did not dwell on present calamities or future dangers. He followed his assessment with an appeal to get to work. He told the people he had the king's authority to enter into a project to rebuild the walls. More importantly, the hand of the Lord was upon him. He cast a vision of possibility if they worked together to rebuild. You know what? The people owned it! They encouraged each other and got to work.

Whatever the level of the repair that needs to take place in your relationship, following deployment, I assure you—God wants to help you make those repairs. Nehemiah saw what he needed to do to restore the city, but he could not do it by himself. You or your husband may see areas in your relationship that need attention. Share your observations with each other and commit to owning together the vision to improve your relationship.

Respond

How would you assess the level of repair that needs to take place in the relationship with your husband following deployment? What is your vision to improve your relationship?

Prayer for the journey

Lord, thank you for my husband. Thank you for allowing us to be together again. Help us to rebuild our relationship in a way that makes it stronger than ever. Give us a godly vision for our marriage. Amen.

Waypoint 20

A family mission

Read

> Next to him Shallum the son of Hallohesh, ruler of half the district of Jerusalem, repaired, he and his daughters. (Nehemiah 3:12)

Reflect

I read Nehemiah chapter 3 and wanted to roll my eyes at the list of names. However, I have studied enough of the Old Testament to recognize their significance and not minimize their effect. As I read this list, I stopped and smiled at the words of Nehemiah 3:12. Don't you love that the daughters of Shallum were right there beside their dad, doing their part to rebuild the wall?

The names in this chapter represent *place* and *responsibility*. Each person and each family had a section that belonged to them and for which they were responsible to repair. Men and women, parents and children, all worked on the wall. Rebuilding became a family project, mission, and goal. No one person's part was over-emphasized as more important. Nehemiah did not bring in expert builders to extend their expert skills. Families worked together to make the repairs in the wall.

That same sense of mission can help when rebuilding your family following a deployment. A shared sense of purpose can be a stimulus for successful reintegration.[29] The establishment of routines and the adjustment of roles may take time and require flexibility. However, if togetherness is the goal, then working together to accomplish that goal gives you a head start.

Age appropriate rebuilding ideas for your family abound. A simple and inexpensive game night can help normalize family relationships through laughter and interaction. If you do not have children, consider an event with extended family. Any positive activity you can do together with family, whether eating together, playing together, or working together, can have a productive outcome.

Respond

"Make repairs" in Nehemiah 3 can also be translated "make strong." How does that change the way you view the lessons in Nehemiah concerning the process of reintegration? What are some positive activities you can plan for your family to build *togetherness*?

Prayer for the journey

Father, thank you for each person in my family. Help us to work together to make our family strong. Amen.

Waypoint 21

Fighting words

Read

> Now when Sanballat heard that we were building the wall, he was angry and greatly enraged, and he jeered at the Jews. And he said in the presence of his brothers and of the army of Samaria, "What are these feeble Jews doing? Will they restore it for themselves? Will they sacrifice? Will they finish up in a day? Will they revive the stones out of the heaps of rubbish, and burned ones at that?" Tobiah the Ammonite was beside him, and he said, "Yes, what they are building—if a fox goes up on it he will break down their stone wall!" Hear, O our God, for we are despised. Turn back their taunt on their own heads and give them up to be plundered in a land where they are captives. (Nehemiah 4:1–4)
>
> So we built the wall. And all the wall was joined together to half its height, for the people had a mind to work. (Nehemiah 4:6)

Reflect

Fighting words. You know them. Someone from outside or inside your walls speak them, and they sting. Fighting words can come in the form of nagging, blaming, criticizing, or venting. Whether you return the punch with your own words or shrink in silent hurt, fighting words are daggers to the soul. Without striking a blow, a word can bring defeat, wreak havoc, and do damage.[30]

The returning exiles were rebuilding. Not happy about the progress, enemies hurled fighting words at Nehemiah and the wall-builders. Naysayers surrounded them, ready to attack. What an intense moment! Outside, enraged enemies; inside, builders frightened by a continual bombardment of propaganda.[31] Would the discouraging words stop the rebuilding effort?

The Israelites organized their army around families. Each family stationed themselves to work, and in this case fight, together. Nehemiah began to muster their courage. He did this out in the open so the enemy could hear and see the preparation for what could have been a minor war.[32]

Can you relate to this war of nerves? You may be making progress in rebuilding your relationship following deployment, and then something discouraging is said, from inside or outside your family walls. Voices whisper, "Too much has changed and your family will never recover." Do not believe the naysayers. Will it take work? Yes! The fact that the words "work" and "fight" are included in this rebuilding scene implies that progress did not come easy. But with God's help, and the will of the families to do the hard work, they made progress—and so can you.

Take heart! Like these builders, muster your family, look to the Lord, ask for his help, and have a mind to work! Even when you are discouraged, don't stop. Look at what you have accomplished, not just what needs to be done. You too can report: "We kept at it, repairing and rebuilding the wall. The whole wall was soon joined together and halfway to its intended height because [our family] had a heart for the work" (Nehemiah 4:6 MSG).

Respond

Have you heard discouraging words from without or within your family concerning redeployment? What strategy can you adopt to fight them from the example in Nehemiah 4?

Prayer for the journey

Father, give my family and me a heart to do the work of rebuilding anything damaged or broken. Help us not to become discouraged, but to keep working together to become the family you have designed. Amen.

Waypoint 22

Multitasking

Read

> From that day on, half of my servants worked on construction, and half held the spears, shields, bows, and coats of mail. And the leaders stood behind the whole house of Judah, who were building on the wall. Those who carried burdens were loaded in such a way that each labored on the work with one hand and held his weapon with the other. (Nehemiah 4:16–17)
>
> And I said to the nobles and to the officials and to the rest of the people, "The work is great and widely spread, and we are separated on the wall, far from one another. In the place where you hear the sound of the trumpet, rally to us there. Our God will fight for us." (Nehemiah 4:19–20)

Reflect

How are you at multitasking? I do not mean eating breakfast and thinking about lunch simultaneously—I have that down to a fine art. Multitasking is the ability to handle more than one task at a time. As much as we value and try to improve our multitasking ability, research reports that it is not good for our bodies or our minds. Yet we continue to challenge the naysayers, and some of us are even successful at holding a sleeping baby with one hand while quietly emptying the dishwasher with the other.

Research does, however, provide strong proof that multitasking can wear you out physically and emotionally.[33] In other words, beware of trying to do too much. Be especially vigilant during the reintegration process. As you focus on rebuilding routine and ritual back into your family, watch for threats like exhaustion and irritability from trying to do it all at one time.

Nehemiah's team of builders put new meaning to multitasking as they worked with one hand with weapons in the other. Their challenge was not only multitasking, but feeling isolated. Each family was responsible for a section of the wall with broad space between each section. It was easy to feel cut off and secluded, to believe the threat of enemy attack was ever-present. To combat the intimidation of "what ifs" Nehemiah established a warning system. The people were to rally to the sound of the trumpet. The builders left no one alone and in danger of ambush.

My friend, you may think you are the only one rebuilding a routine or a relationship while also doing all the other things life demands. But like the Jewish families rebuilding a portion of the city wall, many families in your military community are rebuilding from deployment alongside you.

Sometimes, multitasking is unavoidable. Nehemiah's wall-builders had no choice but to hold a sword in one hand and lay stones with the other. However, they only did this for fifty-two days—until the wall was complete. The days after redeployment may require family multitasking. If all goes well, and with God's help, your family can quickly recover from deployment and shift focus to other family concerns.

Respond

What can you learn from Nehemiah's strategy for completing God's work in Nehemiah 4:9, 14, and 20? In what ways does your family multitask?

Prayer for the journey

Lord, grant me wisdom and courage to face the tasks set before me. When I am weary, remind me: "The eyes of the LORD search the whole earth in order to strengthen those whose hearts are fully committed to him" (2 Chronicles 16:9a NLT). Amen.

Waypoint 23

Hang on

Read

> I also persevered in the work on this wall, and we acquired no land, and all my servants were gathered there for the work. (Nehemiah 5:16)

Reflect

On an empty corner by my house stands a lone tree. For the past year, this tree and what it holds have been a source of encouragement and motivation. Last Christmas some creative soul decorated the tree, brightening an otherwise drab community space. But then the decorations were left to the elements. Month after month, I watched them slowly disappear—except for one lone bulb. For well over a year, that little orb has held on to a branch. Last winter, my area of the country saw its share of wind, rain, and even a hefty deposit of snow. Yet that tiny object holds firm.

I find myself looking for the little sphere of hope as I turn the corner. I anticipate the grief of the day I do not spot it among the branches. There were days I related to it hanging there … alone … exposed … vulnerable … but still hanging on.

I see that same spirit in Nehemiah as he walked out perseverance, sacrifice, and personal integrity in the midst of challenging times. It is the same goal Paul expressed in Colossians 1:9–12. I like the paraphrase from *The Message:*

> … We pray that you'll have the strength to stick it out over the long haul—not the grim strength of gritting your teeth but the glory-strength God gives. It is strength that endures the unendurable and spills over into joy, thanking the Father who makes us strong

enough to take part in everything bright and beautiful that he has for us . . .

The strength Paul refers to is the supernatural *power* of God. The word he uses carries the idea of making strong something or someone that is naturally weak (that's me!)—not a surge of strength but a steady and constant access to Christ, the source of strength. He prayed that we would have strength to stick it out over the long haul—to persevere—to hang in there. He asked the Father to help us remain steadfast under trial without giving in or giving up, no matter the intensity or length of the testing. His prayer covers various trials we may face: sickness, pain, financial loss, death of a loved one, warfare, persecution, marital problems, a wayward child, deployment, reintegration, even a duty station where we just cannot seem to find our place.[34]

Sisters, this is the lesson I learned as I watch the tenacious Christmas bulb: The strength to hang on is not just to hang on. God gives his strength, not just to let us breathe another breath to survive, but to enable us to speak words of hope and encouragement to help others thrive. His strength is not just to help us open our eyes to another dawn, but to help us open our eyes to behold the glory of his majesty all around us. He strengthens us to walk through another day, but that is not where it stops. With God's help, we can climb over obstacles, run and not grow weary, and *"take part in everything bright and beautiful that he has for us."*

Respond

How do you see God's power working in your life to help you hang on? What step forward might God want you to make today?

Prayer for the journey

Lord, thank you for the exchange of your strength for my weakness. Use me to speak words of hope to someone today. Amen.

Waypoint 24

Learning to say no

Read

> Now when Sanballat and Tobiah and Geshem the Arab and the rest of our enemies heard that I had built the wall and that there was no breach left in it (although up to that time I had not set up the doors in the gates), Sanballat and Geshem sent to me, saying, "Come and let us meet together at Hakkephirim in the plain of Ono." But they intended to do me harm. And I sent messengers to them, saying, "I am doing a great work and I cannot come down. Why should the work stop while I leave it and come down to you?" (Nehemiah 6:1–3)

Reflect

Say it with me: *"no."* Come on, you can do better: *"No."* You are almost there. Say it one more time with conviction: *"NO!"* That wasn't so hard, was it? Actually, trust me, I know how hard it can be to say no. Why is that little word such a challenge to get out of a mouth?

In *The Best Yes,* Lysa TerKeurst writes, "Whenever you say yes to something, there is less of you for something else. Make sure your yes is worth the less." She encourages her readers to "Find that courageous yes. Fight for that confident no."[35]

The wall was almost finished. Nehemiah and his team could see the approaching completion of their labor. Then what happened? The enemies of the returning exiles reared their mischievous heads again with an invitation for Nehemiah to meet them. These folks would not take no for an answer. They knew that once Nehemiah finished rebuilding the wall, a political and economic resurgence would occur in the region. They did not want to see a shift in the balance of power that would come with the completed structure. They set out to distract, discredit, and intimidate Nehemiah.[36]

Rebuilding the wall was not something Nehemiah decided to do on a whim. God called him to do the work—a work so significant he could not afford to be distracted. He responded to those who would sidetrack him with a confident "no": "I am doing a great work and I cannot come down. Why should the work stop while I leave it and come down to you?"

When your husband returns from a deployment—short or long—you may be tempted to say, "Good, you're home! Now I can ______________." Oh, but may I issue a caution? Exercise determination to be steadfast in reestablishing your family. Guard against distractions that can keep you from family priorities. Am I encouraging you to say no to everything and only do the family huddle? Of course not, but use wisdom in those things to which you say yes.

Respond

How does 1 Corinthians 15:58 relate to the scene in Nehemiah 6? What can you learn about priorities from Nehemiah's example?

Prayer for the journey

Lord, give me wisdom to discern when to say a confident "no" and the grace to say it with kindness. Guide my family so we do not confuse our priorities. Amen.

Waypoint 25

Done!

Read

> So the wall was finished on the twenty-fifth day of the month Elul, in fifty-two days. And when all our enemies heard of it, all the nations around us were afraid and fell greatly in their own esteem, for they perceived that this work had been accomplished with the help of our God. (Nehemiah 6:15–16)

Reflect

Completed. Finished. Done.

Have you ever worked on a project wondering when you would be able to say those words? Whatever the length, a deployment can feel like it will never be completed, finished, done. Reintegration sometimes bring us to the question, "Are we finished yet?"

Nehemiah and his team of builders completed the work in record time—fifty-two days. Notice the perspective of Nehemiah, ". . . this work had been accomplished with the help of our God." Nehemiah could not attribute the accomplishment to ordinary human effort. The timeframe was impressive, but the timeframe was not the point. God's work on behalf of the people was the point. God was the one who stirred the hearts of people to work, to persevere and finally to prosper.[37]

Nehemiah proclaimed that the wall was completed, but he did not mean the work was done. The same goes for family life. Reaching normalcy does not mean you quit. Keep reading in Nehemiah 6 and you will discover that the hostilities toward the returning Jews continued. Rebuilding the wall was not an end in itself, but it was a step toward continued positive reform for the returning nation.

No one has been able to set parameters and time limits for reintegration following deployment. The goal is to get back to a sense of normalcy. It may happen in fifty-two days—or not. The timeframe is not the goal.

Friend, I write these words to encourage you and remind you that we are people in process. We can never say, "We are done," because we are always facing the next step in the process toward better and stronger. Isn't that what we want for our relationships—with God, with family members, with ourselves?

Respond

How can you relate this quote from Winston Churchill to your family life following deployment? "I have no fear of the future. Let us go forward into its mysteries, let us tear aside the veils that hid it from our eyes, and let us move onward with confidence and courage." In what areas is God calling you to move onward with confidence and courage?

Prayer for the journey

Father, help me to celebrate any sign of a return to normalcy for my family. Let me never settle for thinking we are "done," but keep me moving forward to being better and stronger—always with your help. Amen.

Waypoint 26

Your family name

Read

> Then my God put it into my heart to assemble the nobles and the officials and the people to be enrolled by genealogy. And I found the book of the genealogy of those who came up at the first, and I found written in it: These were the people of the province who came up out of the captivity of those exiles whom Nebuchadnezzar the king of Babylon had carried into exile. They returned to Jerusalem and Judah, each to his town. (Nehemiah 7:5–6)

Reflect

Recently I came across some old military orders my husband had received for a deployment. Not only was his name listed, there was a long list of others who would be deployed with him. His name was on this official record meant more than being one of many to deploy. The list was used to identify those who had access to certain military benefits because of deployment.

Chapter 7 of Nehemiah focuses on a document of names. I know—another list of names, right? The names were representative of lives and history, and being on the list carried with it access to certain benefits as the chosen people of God.

After Nehemiah completed the work on the wall, he turned his attention to the people within the wall. He set out to gather a genealogy of the people to see where different families were living and place some of them in Jerusalem. In order to develop economically, socially, and spiritually, the nation needed people. His research led him to an important genealogical list.[38] He found a record of families who had returned to Jerusalem during the first redeployment. In fact, these names match the names listed in Ezra 2. Nehemiah used the list to remind the people of their identity as a nation. He encouraged them to live their lives in light of their identity.[39]

We can learn a lot about God by looking at the list of names in Nehemiah 7. First, the names listed tell us that God cares about individuals. The names may mean nothing to us, but they sure mean something to God. He knows your name and he sees you with eyes of love and concern.

Second, God cares about families. The list includes some family groups. God has a purpose and a plan for your family. We often question and want to know God's will for the individual, but have you thought about God's will for your family?

Finally, the names show that through all the challenges the exiles experienced, God did not forget them. He returned them to their home and reestablished their purpose. Returning to Jerusalem was not easy, but they were reminded that God had made a promise to their forefather Abraham to give them the Promised Land and that they would be a blessing to the nations around them. God remembered them. This listing of their history reoriented them to both their birthright and their calling.[40]

Note too that we find this listing in God's Word and not just in the administrative records of a nation. It emphasizes the importance God places on individuals and family units.

Respond

In what ways can you strengthen and reestablish the bonds with your extended family, following deployment? What are the challenges? What are the blessings?

Prayer for the journey

Lord, because of your great love for me I can say, "The lines have fallen for me in pleasant places; indeed, I have a beautiful inheritance" (Psalm 16:6). Amen.

Waypoint 27

Joy and strength

Read

> And Nehemiah, who was the governor, and Ezra the priest and scribe, and the Levites who taught the people said to all the people, "This day is holy to the LORD your God; do not mourn or weep." For all the people wept as they heard the words of the Law. Then he said to them, "Go your way. Eat the fat and drink sweet wine and send portions to anyone who has nothing ready, for this day is holy to our Lord. And do not be grieved, for the joy of the LORD is your strength." (Nehemiah 8:9–10)

Reflect

Pictures of new parents with their brand new babies—through birth and adoption—have come across my Facebook news feed this week. The joy on the faces of these parents is undeniable. The little one is not able to respond in kind. The tiny ones are struggling to grow accustomed to their harsh new environment. Their strength to survive and thrive often comes from the joy of the parents. Parental joy motivates a parent to protect, provide, and nurture their child's full potential.

In Nehemiah 8, Ezra read God's Word to the community. As the holy words poured forth, the sound of weeping rose among those gathered. The people grieved as the light of truth dawned on them. They realized their sin of disobedience, neglect, and lack of commitment as God's people. Instead of chastising them, Ezra and the priests told the people not to grieve because *"the joy of the LORD is [their] strength."*

Many years prior, the prophet Zephaniah exhorted the people to rejoice at the restoration of Jerusalem (Zephaniah 3:14–20). He proclaimed that the Lord would be in their midst and he would rejoice over them. Now Nehemiah encouraged the people to rejoice in knowing God's delight in them was more significant than their failure to follow the law. God's good pleasure had stirred the heart of the king who allowed the Jews to return to their land to reconstruct their temple, to rebuild their city wall, and now to restore their people. God took great delight in this restoration process.[41] The people could be strong because God took joy in them.

As you put your trust in the Lord, you will receive the strength that comes from our heavenly Father. Trusting in him results in confidence that he will provide for your family's needs, protect your family relationships, and help your family accomplish what you cannot achieve on your own. Let the joy of the Lord give you strength to move through the stages of reintegration and beyond.

Respond

Ezra reminded the returning exiles that their joy was to be in God's provision for them. How have you and your family experienced joy in the Lord during deployment? What encouragement do you find in the words of Zephaniah 3:14–20?

Prayer for the journey

Father, my source of strength is not in independence, self-discipline, talents, or abilities. My strength is not in my husband, children, or friends. My strength is not in national superiority or military might. My strength is in you. Let me live in daily recognition that my help comes from you. Amen.

Waypoint 28

Build a booth

Read

> On the second day the heads of fathers' houses of all the people, with the priests and the Levites, came together to Ezra the scribe in order to study the words of the Law. And they found it written in the Law that the LORD had commanded by Moses that the people of Israel should dwell in booths during the feast of the seventh month, and that they should proclaim it and publish it in all their towns and in Jerusalem, "Go out to the hills and bring branches of olive, wild olive, myrtle, palm, and other leafy trees to make booths, as it is written." So the people went out and brought them and made booths for themselves, each on his roof, and in their courts and in the courts of the house of God … And all the assembly of those who had returned from the captivity made booths and lived in the booths, for from the days of Jeshua the son of Nun to that day the people of Israel had not done so. And there was very great rejoicing. (Nehemiah 8:13–17)

Reflect

A tongue-in-cheek joke told during overseas assignments goes like this: "Why do U.S. military serving overseas smile more than the local nationals? They have a DEROS."[42] Military life is one of the best reminders of the temporary nature of life. A deployment will end, a PCS[43] will happen, an assignment will change, a neighbor will move—and then this cycle will begin again. If you are unhappy with a person, a house, or a situation at one assignment, just smile and wait for the inevitable change that will come.

I know military wives who have a hard time viewing life through the lens of *temporary.* They struggle to adjust to the constant change. I know others who embrace the opportunity to experience new things.

God's Word reminded these Jews of the temporary nature of life. They renewed the celebration of the Feast of Booths by building temporary shelters that replicated the tents of their ancestors' wilderness wanderings with Moses. They rejoiced together as a community over the grace of God that kept their families intact during the years of wandering. God not only sustained them, but also returned them to the land of promise.[44]

A temporary view of life is a biblical view of life. This is not a morbid or melancholic focus. It is realistic, and for the Christ-follower it is hopeful. We have an eternal view. This world is not our permanent home. Just as the Feast of Booths reminded the Jews of God's provision and care in a transitional state, we can be confident the Lord is with us and will help us through all our transitions. Reintegration is an important transition, but for a career military family it is one of many temporary transitions.

Here's an idea. In your mind, build a booth for reintegration to remind you God is with you. Later you may want to build a PCS booth, a new assignment booth, or a deployment booth. Each time, reflect with your family on how God helped you through the last transition and how he will help you through this one.

Respond

What can we learn about the temporary nature of life from Ecclesiastes 3:11 and James 4:13–16? Which military experiences remind you of the temporary nature of this life?

Prayer for the journey

Lord, give me an eternal perspective. Give me a grateful heart and a joyful spirit in this temporary life. Help me make the most of every opportunity. Amen. (See Colossians 4:5)

Waypoint 29

Sign on the dotted line

Read

"Now, therefore, our God, the great, the mighty, and the awesome God, who keeps covenant and steadfast love, let not all the hardship seem little to you that has come upon us, upon our kings, our princes, our priests, our prophets, our fathers, and all your people, since the time of the kings of Assyria until this day." (Nehemiah 9:32)

"Because of all this we make a firm covenant in writing; on the sealed document are the names of our princes, our Levites, and our priests." (Nehemiah 9:38)

"We will not neglect the house of our God." (Nehemiah 10:39b)

Reflect

Renewal of vows is the focus of Weddings for Warriors. The nonprofit organization, founded in Savannah by Becky and James Byous, seeks to celebrate military marriages that remain firm despite the challenges. Each year, hundreds of volunteers provide their services and supplies to help military couples remember the priority of their marriage.[45] I have never attended a renewal of marriage vows, but I can imagine it is a meaningful and moving event. Family members publicly vowing to love and value one another is powerful.

Chapter 10 of Nehemiah reads almost like a renewal of vows. As a nation, the Jewish people looked back to previous spiritual journeys. Together, they vowed total allegiance to what God said to them through the covenant made with Moses, "to follow the Law of God … and to obey carefully all the commands, regulations, and decrees of the Lord our God."[46] The covenant was both a personal and corporate commitment that people signed, sealed, and recorded. They publicly testified to their neighbors that they were presenting themselves afresh to God. This covenant held specific and precise promises because true renewal cannot succeed on sweeping statements and vague declarations.[47] This covenant got to the nitty-gritty details of marriage, money, and worship.

The people of God purposed to make their commitment more than just a new desire; they purposed to show their commitment through renewed action.[48] This was an opportunity to start fresh and get it right—to make changes and adjustments.

A renewal of vows can be lovely and meaningful, but is not necessary to renew the commitment you and your family have for God and for each other. In what ways do you desire to start fresh in your commitment to one another?

Respond

Consider writing and signing a family covenant. Affixing a name to an agreement can be a public declaration of intent and can serve as a means for accountability.

Prayer for the journey

Thank you, Lord, for the hope that comes from knowing and serving you. Help my family to be committed to loving, honoring and serving you. Make our commitment to you and one another strong and sure. Amen.

Waypoint 30

A walk around the wall

Read

> Then I brought the leaders of Judah up onto the wall and appointed two great choirs that gave thanks. (Nehemiah 12:31a)
>
> And the joy of Jerusalem was heard far away. (Nehemiah 12:43b)

Reflect

Read Chapter 12 closely and get a picture of Nehemiah as an impressive orchestrator. The description of music and choreography might rival a wholesome Super Bowl halftime show. The grand display of synchronized movement did not overshadow the unrestrained joy of the celebration.[49] The returning Jews dedicated this day to giving thanks to God for his provision and his goodness. The city was rebuilt and would now be dedicated as a place where God would be worshipped, followed, and made known.[50]

Similar to the way military leaders today proudly conduct a ceremonial inspection during a change of command, Nehemiah took city leaders on a walk around the wall. This was the wall that enemies said could not hold a fox (Nehemiah 4:3). Now choirs marched atop in song. This was the wall naysayers said could not be rebuilt. Now leaders of the city stood on top for inspection.

Friend, you may have thought your family would not survive deployment—but you did. You may think your family cannot survive reintegration—but you can. By the help of the Lord, your family can bring others to the top of your rebuilt wall to show what you can accomplish through faith in God. Will you steward the opportunity you have as a military family to be an example of God's faithfulness?

A note of caution: Chapter 12 celebrates the accomplishment of rebuilding. Unfortunately, Chapter 13 reveals that the people did not follow up their celebration with a continued commitment to serve God. As life went on and Nehemiah returned to Persia, the people of Jerusalem became lax in their commitment. As you complete this thirty-day journey of hope, celebrate the good God has done and is going to do in your family, and be determined to keep your commitments to your family and to the Lord.

Respond

If you have ever been involved in a dedication for a marriage, baby, military, or church building, reflect on what makes such a ceremony special and significant. Consider planning a mini-family reunion or a special meal with friends and families to celebrate God's goodness to your family.

Prayer for the journey

Lord, thank you for your sustaining grace and mercy. Help my family to be surrendered to your constant work in our lives—as individuals and as a family. Keep us humble and gracious in our interactions with one another, and help us be an example of what you can do in and through a family committed to serving you. Amen.

Notes for Journey 1

1. John Goldingay, *Baker Commentary on the Old Testament Wisdom and Psalms: Volume 3* (Grand Rapids: Baker Academic Books, 2008), 47.
2. Temper Longman III, *How to Read Exodus* (Downers Grove, IL: IVP Academic, 2009), 102.
3. William H. C. Propp, *Exodus 1–18 The Anchor Yale Bible Commentaries* (New Haven, CT: Yale University Press, 1999), 200.
4. Peter Enns, *Exodus: The NIV Application Commentary* (Grand Rapids: Zondervan, 2000), 55.
5. Douglas Stuart, *Exodus: An Exegetical and Theological Exposition of Holy Scripture* (Nashville, TN: Broadman & Holman, 2006), 119.
6. Enns, 161.
7. Stuart, 169.
8. Stuart, 283.
9. Ibid, 273.
10. Enns, 13.
11. James K. Bruckner, *Exodus: Understanding the Bible Commentary Series* (Grand Rapids: Baker Books, 2008), 5.
12. Ibid, 7.
13. Enns, 25.
14. "Dealing with Deployment," www.military.com, http://www.military.com/spouse/military-deployment/dealing-with-deployment/deployment-family-rituals (accessed November 18, 2014).
15. Enns, 279.
16. Kristen Welch, *Rhinestone Jesus: Saying Yes to God When Sparkly, Safe Faith is No Longer Enough* (Nashville, TN: Tyndale Momentum, 2014), 11.
17. Stuart, 326.
18. Ennes, 270.

19. Tom Hale and Steve Thorson, *Applied Old Testament Commentary* (Colorado Spring, CO: David C. Cook, 2007), 229.

20. Daniel Gurtner, *Exodus: A Commentary of the Greek Text of Codex Vaticunus* (The Netherlands: Brill Publishing, 2013), 330.

21. Victor P. Hamilton, *Exodus: An Exegetical Commentary* (Grand Rapids: Baker Academic, 2011), 211.

22. Enns, 273.

23. Thomas B. Dozeman, *Eerdmans Critical Commentary: Exodus* (Grand Rapids: Wm B. Eerdmans, 2009), 328.

24. Catherine Clark Kroeger and Mary J. Evans, editors, *IVP Women's Bible Commentary* (Downers Grove, ILL: InterVarsity Press, 2002), 36.

25. Enns, 307.

26. Hale and Thorson, 232.

27. "The Story of 'Grace.'" http://www.gracebyenstrom/history.htms (accessed November 20, 2014)..

28. Hamilton, 255.

29. Bruckner, 3.

30. Brevard S. Childs, *The Book of Exodus: A Critical, Theological Commentary* (Louisville, KY: Westminster John Knox Press, 1974), 292.

31. Stacy Bannerman, "Multiple Deployments May Raise Risk of Military Spouse Suicide," www.truth-out.org/archive/item/ 86547:multiple-deployments-may-raise-risk-of-military-spouse-suicide, (accessed November 22, 2014).

32. Hamilton, 258.

33. Ronald Clements, *The Cambridge Bible Commentary on the New English Bible: Exodus* (London: Cambridge University Press, 1972), 103.

34. Hamilton, 272.

35. Enns, 489.

36. Gordon J. Wenham, J. Alec Motyer, Donald A. Carson, R. T. France, editors, *The New Bible Commentary* (Downers Grove, ILL: InterVarsity Academic Press, 1994), 131.

37. Roger Roy, "Survival Tips for Families of POW's: Vietnam Officer's Wife Offers Advice," *Orlando Sentinel*, January 19, 1991, http://articles.orlandosentinel.com/1991–01–19/news/9101190846_1_vietnam-war-pows-north-vietnam, (accessed December 8, 2014).

38. *The New Bible Commentary*, 137.

39. Benno Jacob, *The Second Book of the Bible: Exodus* (Jersey City, New Jersey: Ktav Publishing, 1992), 966.

40. *The New Bible Commentary*, 138.

41. Bob Deffenbaugh, "The Presence of God with his People (Exodus 33:12–17)," www.bible.org, accessed December 9, 2014. https://bible.org/seriespage/28-presence-god-his-people-exodus-3312–17.

42. She of the Sea, "The Angry Stage of Deployment, http://spousebuzz.com/blog/2009/11/the-angry-stage-of deployment.html #ixzz3LVN-wV9bX (accessed December 10, 2014).

43. William Elwell, *Evangelical Dictionary of Biblical Theology* (Grand Rapids: Baker Publishing Group, 1996), 1166.

Notes for Journey 2

1. https://lumina.bible.org/bible/Ezra+1 Hebrew definition.
2. "For thus says the Lord: When seventy years are completed for Babylon, I will visit you, and I will fulfill to you my promise and bring you back to this place" (Jeremiah 29:10).
3. Kathy Dahlen and Knute Larson, *Holman Old Testament Commentary: Ezra, Nehemiah, Esther* (Nashville, TN: B&H Publishing Group, 2005), 8.
4. Bruce Feiler, "The Stories that Bind Us" *New York Times* March 15, 2013, http://www.nytimes.com/2013/03/17/fashion/the-family-stories-that-bind-us-this-life.html?_r=0
5. Dahlen and Larson, *Holman OT Commentary*, 25.
6. King Solomon built the first temple, which became the preeminent symbol of national and religious unity for the nation of Israel. The Babylonians destroyed this temple in 587 B.C.
7. John F. Walvoord and Roy B. Zuck, *The Bible Knowledge Commentary: Old Testament* (Colorado Springs: David C. Cook, 1983), 658.
8. Keith N. Schoville, *The College Press NIV Commentary: Ezra-Nehemiah* (Joplin, MO: College Press Publishing, 2001), 66.
9. Lydia I. Marek, "Returning home: What we know about the reintegration of deployed service members into their families and communities," https://www.ncfr.org/ncfr-report/focus/military-families/returning-home.
10. 2 Chronicles 5:13
11. Catherine Clark Kroeger and Mary J. Evans, editors, *The IVP Women's Bible Commentary* (Downers Grove, ILL: InterVarsity Press, 2002), 249.
12. Mark D. Roberts, *The Preacher's Commentary, Volume 11: Ezra, Nehemiah, Esther* (Nashville, TN: Thomas Nelson, 2002), 72.
13. Robert Fyall, *The Message of Ezra and Haggai* (Downers Grove, ILL: InterVarsity Press, 2010), 80.
14. Ibid, 81.

15. F. Charles Fensham, *The New International Commentary of the Old Testament: Ezra-Nehemiah* (Grand Rapids, MI: William B. Eerdmans, 1982), 99.

16. Jacey Eckhart, "7 Things I Wish I'd Known About Military Marriage," *Spousebuzz Blog,* March 22, 2012, http://spousebuzz.com/blog/2012/03/7-things-i-wish-id-known-about-military-marriage.html, (accessed March 3, 2015).

17. "Divorce Study: Financial Arguments Early in Relationships May Predict Divorce," Huff Post, July 12, 2013, http://www.huffingtonpost.com/2013/07/12/divorce-study_n_3587811.html, (accessed March 5, 2015).

18. Leslie C. Allen and Timothy S. Laniak, *Understanding the Bible Commentary Series: Ezra, Nehemiah, Esther* (Grand Rapids, MI: Baker Books, 2003), 74.

19. Ralph Davis, "Ezra-Nehemiah: Part 7," *IIIM Magazine Online* 2, no. 50 (December 2000): 1, http://thirdmill.org/newfiles/ral_davis/OT.Davis.Ezra.9.pdf., (accessed March 5, 2015).

20. Dahlen and Larson, *Holman OT Commentary,* 105.

21. David X. Cifu and Cory Blake, "Post Deployment Syndrome: The Illness of War," http://www.brainlinemilitary.org/content/2011/03/post-deployment-syndrome-the-illness-of-war_pageall.html, (accessed March 5, 2015).

22. Allen and Laniak, *Understanding the Bible,* 75.

23. Fensham, *NICOT,* 128.

24. Ralph Davis, "God's People in Gray Times," *IIIM Magazine Online* 2, no. 45 (November, 2000), 2, http://thirdmill.org/articles/ral_davis/OT.Davis.Ezra.3.pdf. (accessed March 8, 2015)

25. Fensham, *NICOT,* 130.

26. Steven L. Sayers, "Family Reintegration Difficulties and Couples Therapy for Military Veterans and Their Spouses," *Cognitive and Behavioral Practice* 18, no. 1 (February 2011): 110, http://psycnet.apa.org/psycinfo/2010-15791-001, (accessed March 6, 2015).

27. Allen & Laniak, *NIBC: Ezra, Nehemiah, Esther,* 99.

28. Fensham, *NICOT,* 167.

29. Mark C. Pisano, "Military Deployment and Family Reintegration," National Association of School Psychologists, Wounded Vet Center, University of Illinois, http://woundedvetcenter.ahs.illinois.edu/pdf/Military_Deployment_and_Family_Reintegration.pdf, (accessed March 7, 2015).

30. Julia Schemmer, "The Power of Words," *Huff Post*, January 22, 2014, http://www.huffingtonpost.com/julia-schemmer/the-power-of-words_b_4516603.html, (accessed March 6, 2015).

31. Fensham, *NICOT*, 186.

32. Ibid.

33. "Multitasking: Switching Costs," www.apa.org, March 20, 2006, http://www.apa.org/research/action/multitask.aspx, (accessed March 7, 2015).

34. J. Hampton Keathley, III, "Four Ways to Walk in a Manner Worthy of the Lord (Colossians 1:10b-12a)," https://bible.org/seriespage/four-ways-walk-manner-worthy-lord-col-110b-12a, (accessed March 8, 2015).

35. Lysa TerKeurst, *The Best Yes* (Nashville, TN: Thomas Nelson, 2014), 35.

36. Allen and Laniak, *NIBC: Ezra, Nehemiah, Esther,* 113.

37. Hamilton, *Exalting Jesus in Ezra-Nehemiah,* 145.

38. Fensham, *NICOT,* 211.

39. Steven J. Cole, "Lesson 7: Counting for God (Nehemiah 7:1–73)," https://bible.org/seriespage/lesson-7-counting-god-nehemiah-71–73, (accessed March 8, 2015).

40. Derek Kidner, *Ezra & Nehemiah, Tyndale Old Testament Commentaries* (Downers Grove, ILL: InterVarsity Academic, 2009), 103.

41. Hamilton, *Exalting Jesus in Ezra-Nehemiah,* 158.

42. DEROS is an acronym for Date Eligible for Return from Overseas.

43. PCS is an acronym for Permanent Change of Station.

44. Hamilton, *Exalting Jesus in Ezra-Nehemiah,* 151.

45. Military couples wed, renew vows in Savannah through Weddings for Warriors Posted: January 14, 2015 - 10:56pm, http://savannahnow.com/news/2015–01–14/military-couples-wed-renew-vows-savannah-through-weddings-warriors

46. Raymond Brown, *The Message of Nehemiah* (Downers Grove, IL: InterVarsity Press, 1998), 173.

47. Ralph Davis, "Ezra-Nehemiah: Part 17," *IIIM Magazine Online* 3, No. 25 (June 2001), 4, http://thirdmill.org/magazine/article.asp/link/http:^^thirdmill.org^ articles^ral_davis^OT.Davis.Neh.10.html/at/Ezra-Nehemiah,%20part%2017 (accessed March 7, 2015)

48. Dahlen and Larson, *Holman OT Commentary,* 247.

49. Ibid, 260.

50. Hamilton, *Exalting Jesus in Ezra-Nehemiah,* 207.

Thank you for coming along with Brenda on this encounter with God's Word!

We pray that God will continue to encourage you in the next season of your life. To continue your journey in Scripture, look for the other books in this series:

- **Dedicated: Steps of Faith in God's Plan**
- **Devoted: Steps of Love Toward Healthy Relationships**
- **Deployed: Steps of Hope in Times of Uncertainty**
- **Directed: Steps of Peace in Times of Transition**

You can find them, along with other small group materials and resources to start your own online community at **www.MilitaryWife.bible.**

You can also order free copies of these books for other military wives at **ArmedServicesMinistry.com.**

We need your help... How has God's Word impacted your life?

Dear Military Wife,

American Bible Society is honored to share this Journey with you! Thank you for your selfless devotion to your husband and our country.

Generous contributions from our supporters make it possible for us to provide these resources to you free of charge. As a way of thanking these faithful supporters, we love to share stories of how our Scripture resources have made a difference in someone's life.

Please take a moment to fill out the postage-paid card to the right and share how this Journey has impacted your life.

You may provide us with your name or remain anonymous.

Thank you and God bless you!

Annie LoCastro
Armed Services Ministry Program Manager
Email: **Provisions@AmericanBible.org**

Check out our website for other devotions:
www.MilitaryWife.bible

JOURNEY OF A MILITARY WIFE: DEPLOYED

In what branch of service does (or did) your husband serve?

____

Check current status:
☐ **ACTIVE DUTY** ☐ **RESERVES/NATIONAL GUARD** ☐ **VETERAN**

This Journey has positively influenced my perception of the Bible and its message for me and my family.
☐ **YES** ☐ **NO**

Did this Journey encourage you to further explore the Bible and God's promises?
☐ **YES** ☐ **NO**

Did you read through this Journey as part of a group or study?
☐ **YES** ☐ **NO**

How has this Journey helped you better apply the Bible to your life? What positive action did you take?

____

____

____

☐ **YES** ☐ **NO**
I would like someone from the American Bible Society to contact me so I can share my story on how this Scripture resource has impacted my life. *Someone will* ***ONLY*** *contact you* ***if*** *the Yes space is checked.*

____
NAME

____
ADDRESS LINE 1

____
ADDRESS LINE 2

____
TELEPHONE **EMAIL**

Tear here before mailing

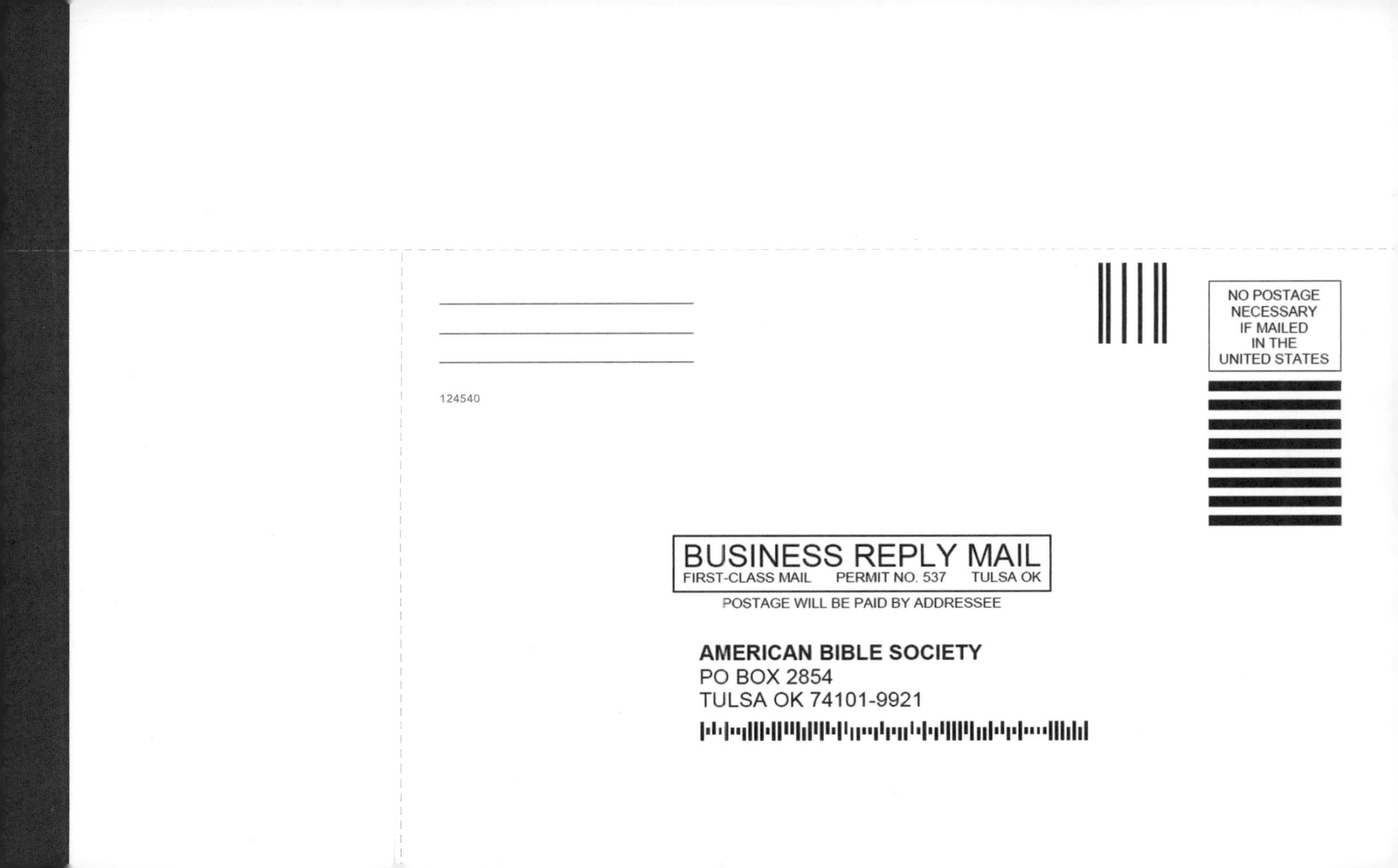
NO POSTAGE
NECESSARY
IF MAILED
IN THE
UNITED STATES
124540
BUSINESS REPLY MAIL
FIRST-CLASS MAIL PERMIT NO. 537 TULSA OK
POSTAGE WILL BE PAID BY ADDRESSEE
AMERICAN BIBLE SOCIETY
PO BOX 2854
TULSA OK 74101-9921